Remember Me

Remember Me

A Holocaust Survivor's Story

Marian Kampinski

iUniverse, Inc.
New York   Bloomington

Remember Me
A Holocaust Survivor's Story

iUniverse books may be ordered through booksellers or by contacting:

iUniverse
1663 Liberty Drive
Bloomington, IN 47403
www.iuniverse.com
1-800-Authors (1-800-288-4677)

Because of the dynamic nature of the Internet, any Web addresses or links contained in this book may have changed since publication and may no longer be valid. The views expressed in this work are solely those of the author and do not necessarily reflect the views of the publisher, and the publisher hereby disclaims any responsibility for them.

ISBN: 978-1-4401-2178-4 (pbk)
ISBN: 978-1-4401-2177-7 (dj)
ISBN: 978-1-4401-2179-1 (ebk)

Printed in the United States of America

iUniverse rev. date: 1/27/2009

This book is dedicated to my family,
to the millions who lost their lives in the Holocaust,
and to the survivors who suffered along with them.

The Tree of Life Continues

Thanks to God that our tree of life continues through our children, grandchildren, and great grandchildren, and through future generations to come. My husband Isak and I currently reside happily in Cleveland, Ohio. My devoted son Chuck, who was so instrumental in helping to put this book together, also resides in Cleveland. His children are Lisa and David. Lisa and her husband Allen Ehrlich have a son named Camden Sage and have recently welcomed into the world their second son, Indigo Wren.

My oldest daughter, Nancy currently lives with her husband Shaul Saginahor in Israel. Their children are Shira and Zehava. My younger daughter, Chana Anita Mosbacher, and her husband Rabbi Yaakov Mosbacher also live in Israel. Their children are Moshe, David, Yossi, Tzipporah, Shloimi, Yoheved, Bezalel, Shmuel, Benjamin, and Hadassah. My youngest son, Jack lives in Cleveland as well.

Table of Contents

Life Is A Gift

I asked of Death
What is death
And death was silent
And motionless

And then I asked of Life
What is life
And life took me
On a journey

And I came to
an understanding
(by living it)

Introduction

By nature I am a poet. I see the poetry and the beauty in everything around me. I see it in the faces of my family, my children and their children. I see it in the calm, tree-lined Cleveland street that greets me every dawn for my morning walk to the bench by the fountain at the nearby mall where I write my poetry. I see it when my memories of the horrors and the triumphs of survival that I have witnessed fill the pages of my notebook. The seeds of this memoir were planted years ago with the suggestion of a trusted friend who had been stirred by some poems I'd written and read at a dedication for the Holocaust Memorial at the Zion Cemetery in Cleveland.

It was a cold, gray morning and a crowd of hundreds–survivors, their families, and others–had gathered at the cemetery to remember those who were murdered. The ceremony began as planned with a formal procession, followed by a moving introductory speech by Simon Fixler, the chairman of the Jewish survivor's organization in Cleveland called *Kol Israel*. After Simon's speech, six survivors lit six commemorative candles – one for each million gone, and rabbi Shubert Spero of the Young Israel Congregation addressed the audience, speaking to issues of the Holocaust both past and present. Then a cantor, Leonard Fuchs, another survivor, sang a stirring *El Malai Rachamin*, the traditional memorial prayer that asks God to gather up the souls of the departed into eternal life. Toward the end of the ceremony, I went to the podium and recited my poems. I remember looking out at the audience as I read. Many were drying their tears, sobbing audibly. When it was over, my friends congratulated me, thanked me for reading, and encouraged me to write more.

Writing the poems that I read that morning had been difficult and trying. Previously, I had never attempted to write about my years in the Łódź ghetto and concentration camps. A kind of protective forgetting had settled over me after May 3, 1945, the day of my liberation. Silence became my comfort. It functioned like a calmative against the unspeakable nature of those memories. But after hearing some of my other poems read aloud at our group gatherings, my husband and friends in Kol Israel convinced me to put down in poetry my experience of the Holocaust.

I thought about it and decided that I did want to speak for the many who wouldn't or couldn't, but the challenge of putting words to the unspeakable felt terribly daunting. Talking about those years was difficult enough. When approached with questions about my time in the ghetto and concentration camps, I would usually avoid the subject, or try to change it to something else. Even in conversation with my children, I avoided talking about it. They were innocent and I wanted to shelter them from the suffering I had faced. My brother Icek, my sister Etka, beloved cousins and friends, and I had been thrust immediately into a world of oppression, affliction, and survival, forced to grow up practically overnight. Every child was exposed to the worst evils and lost their innocence in a heartbeat. As memories linger, and after I had written a few poems, I was to write this poem:

Innocence

In beauty did she walk
Purity was her tower
Dressed in white
Like a wedding bride
In freshness spring to flower

In the world of innocence
She walked in grace
And cradled her dreams
Of values to be praised
Her virtues of essence
Of honor and pride
Treasured her life
Of freedom that coincides

Then shadows of darkness
Befell her world she lived
Swift changes of madness
Sorrow and sadness
By Nazi's rules most evil decrees
All was lost humanity ceased

Nonstop gas chambers ignited
Burning flesh choking tears
Sealed walls for no one to hear
Chimneys, smoke, smell
Sickness in the air
As all helplessly died in despair

Her pure soul cries out
For mankind, love of concern
Return, return, let innocence return
Let justice and righteousness
Be your life to endure
To dwell in the world of peace
To be safe and secure

With my children, especially when they were young, I sometimes felt like I regained some of my own lost childhood innocence. In protecting them from the stories of my life, I wondered if I wasn't also protecting myself. Eventually, I found myself seriously contemplating the suggestion of writing the poem. It was late in the evening and I had put my children to bed. I began to clear the table as usual, to straighten the dining room a little, and turn off lights. Then I sat down in an armchair to relax and clear my mind.

As I sat down, I caught a glimpse of the sideboard that took up the length of one dining room wall. I turned and stared at the drawers. Inside the drawers were our family photo albums. Before I knew it, the drawers were opened and the albums were cradled in my arms. I walked slowly over to the dining room table, eased into a chair, opened an album to the first few pages and stared at the photos. There they were, the children, my sons and two daughters, pictures of them happily playing on the front lawn, or smiling behind a candle-lit birthday cake, or standing with Mother, their *Bubbe*, next to a lake. I felt peaceful doing this and joyful. I felt blessed to have my children and the photos that recorded their growth from year to year.

Smiling, I turned the pages one by one, lightly touching the photos as each set of three or four passed under to the next page. As I did this, I found myself facing a strange but pleasant awareness of what my survival meant. My survival meant my children's survival and their children's survival. I realized then how important my children were to me. I realized also at that moment how much my mother had done for me, and how much she was still with me. All her life, through the most extreme and arduous of situations, she was a role model for how to love and protect your family.

I closed the albums and put them back in the drawer intending to go to bed. The house had grown peaceful, hushed except for the muted hum of the refrigerator. Everyone was asleep or in his or her room, but I was restless. I sat back down at the table and thought of the moments of my life that those photos depicted. I recalled good times and bad, the struggles as well as the successes. Then abruptly and without warning, like a flashing nightmare, images of the Holocaust appeared: my father leaving to escape the Nazi persecution; the tiny over-stuffed Ghetto rooms; the transport trains; the concentration camp barracks; the barbed wire fences; the barking dogs; the shouting guards and their whips and guns; the bitter cold, the gaunt, typhus-ravaged and hunger-stricken bodies; the patchy shaved heads, the unfitted clothes hanging loosely over emaciated shoulders, the ghostly faces of the *Musselman*—the ones who had nothing left emotionally or physically and had given up. Worst of all, I suddenly saw in front of me what I hadn't seen since the last day I exited the barracks at Stutthof in 1945–hundreds of dead bodies piled high one on top of the other, as if put there by a perverse sculptor. Before my wide eyes played a grotesque dance of horror.

Those years haunted me. Every day I was hunted. Sitting at the table, I was haunted and hunted all over again. When living through those years, I was too mortified and taken over by the constant randomness of survival and anxiety of day-to-day life to cry. Everything was about survival. There was no time for sentiment. The Nazis plundered our lives and beat us into numbness. We became numb to the chaos, numb to the violence, numb to the death and disease. What could we do? They had tyrannical power over our bodies. Any inward movement, any stirring of the spirit to action was a signal that their power was not absolute, a signal that they may have stripped us of our outward Jewish identity, confined and crushed our bodies, and muted our humanity, but they had not robbed us of our spirit or our being.

At that quiet moment, late at night, what had been locked inside me for years, frozen like ice, began to melt. All the memories came back, even the good memories of people's heroism and compassion amid the worst, most inhuman conditions. A huge burden welled up from which I immediately had to be free. Slowly, the tears began to pour from my eyes. I grabbed a notepad and pen and started to write. Once begun, I could not stop. With each watery tear dropping onto the yellow paper below, a little more of the burden lifted. I kept writing until, on the blotchy paper below, was a poem. "We Cannot Forget" it was called. It was after midnight. Upon its completion, I went to the living room and fell asleep on the couch.

We Cannot Forget

We cry and cry,
We can't stop crying
Recalling our loved ones –
The way they were dying.
Children were born – being abused –
Exterminated – tortured.
Our crime – we were Jews!
They went on feasting,
Being amused,
While more and more gas chambers
Were being used.
Days with sorrow.
Nights with pain,
We were driven
Sick – insane.

Spring came,
But it was not the same,
Not a spring once known,
Of fragrant flowers.
The smell of chimneys
Took over.
We were choking,
But the chimneys
Went on smoking.

There was a summer,
Not of warmth and growth,
Like the ones we so loved.
There was a summer of
Hunger and thirst.
Dry, weak and wearied
We surrendered – at first.

There was an autumn,
Not like the ones we recall
When the trees were bare and
Colorful leaves would fall.
There was an autumn,
For falling, withering Jews
Raked like leaves –
No more of use.

There was a winter
Without children at play,
When snowflakes were falling,
Once carefree voices – joyful calling.
There was winter
Of slaughtered flesh,
Warm blood and cold ashes
Scattered all over –
A bloodshed cover.
Those were the seasons

Of burning hell.
We were there and
We can tell.

We cry and cry,
For we were hurt so deep,
For no reason and
In the prime of the season
Forever we weep –
For the loss of joy,
For all those girls and boys,
For those fathers and mothers,
For those sisters and brothers,
For all six million,
Caught in a net,
Their eternal silence
We can't forget.

Though there is hope for a tree,
Never more will you bloom or be.
Left is only the memory of you,
May you sleep in peace.
May your life of pain,
Be not in vain.
May we be guided
To a better tomorrow,
And each coming generation
Never know such tragic sorrow.

The entire next day the thoughts and images continued to creep into my mind. That night I ended up at the dining room table once more with a pen in my hand, writing new lines with every set of tears. The words would open wounds and splash them onto the page, then, for a brief moment, the wounds would close and heal a little. From this, another poem arose, "Galloping Flames of Fire."

Galloping Flames of Fire

I began to blossom, like in spring,
And I felt like a bird – to fly and sing.
I thought of joy that life would bring,
Instead of wounds and broken wings.
Robbed was I, when young of age,
Forced into a ghetto cage,
Zoned with barbed wire,
Where I felt the flames of fire.

The German Nazi's rise
Was powerful –
Full of corruption –
Limitless destruction.
In a rage of blazing fury,
Nazi's were the judge and jury.
Driving crimes of desire
Galloping flames of fire.

Encompassing the roads were the devils –
With waves of hell,
Destroying synagogues,
Crumbling they fell
To be of worship no more.
In vain I wept for vanished time
When the synagogues were shining
With lights sublime,
Glowing from the sacred Torah,
Every corner filled with prayers,
Exalted synagogues – everywhere.

I was but a teenager,
But grew older overnight.
In spite of my aching age,
To survive was my fight.

And I hoped to escape
From the German murderer's rape.
And my eyes in supplication lifted,
For a miracle I prayed.

The German crimes went on,
There was no place to hide or run.
Growing horror, misery and defeat,
Swollen faces, swollen feet.
From hunger, sickness and disease
Death was everyday increased.
Out cried agony and sorrow –
No hope left for tomorrow.

In continued raids,
The Germans pushed through ghetto gates,
In a hunt for young and old
To be shipped in freight wagons
Thirsty, hungry and cold.
Children were sick and weak,
Fearing to cry or speak,
Sent to be slaughtered – like lamb
In concentration camps.

In the last of strength,
The last struggle at length,
In the ghetto's echoed cry –
Live or die!
United in thought,
Up rose a ghetto and fought.
Though in bloodshed and ruins,
Spirit ran high –
No more afraid.

Gallant and brave –
Where everyone served,
Side by side

In honor and pride.
In one last strike for freedom –
Burst asunder the barbed wire
And died fighting
The flames of fire.

I recall a dream I had as a child. I was about eleven years old. I stood high above the sky. There was vastness, darkness and empty space all around me. Alone, frightened, unable to move or escape, a nurse suddenly appeared in a shaft of light ahead of me. She was pushing forward an old man hunched over in a wheelchair. He had a gaunt, sickly face, with deep shadows marking the crevices in his skin. His legs were covered down to his feet with two gray blankets. The nurse stopped and pointed at the man. I didn't know why she was pointing. I thought she was trying to show me how miserable he looked. Then a voice spoke, but the voice didn't come from the man or the nurse. "Never forget," it said. "Never forget," it repeated.

I didn't know what to forget or not to forget. All I knew was that I was standing there in the darkness and all of a sudden it was hard to breathe and then I woke up. Maybe the dream had nothing to do with anything, or maybe it had something to do with those poor souls who were just evaporated and whose story I could tell in telling my own. Of course, as many dreams do, this dream didn't let me rest. It stayed with me many years. Eventually I related it to my experience as a survivor. So, like the nurse demanded, I didn't forget and, remembering the dream, wrote the poem, *Blackened Skies*:

Blackened Skies

Tremble earth tremble
For judgment is near
As God is our witness
He will judge you for your crimes
And atrocities committed
By all means of evil
You gassed, you murdered, you slaughtered

Tremble earth tremble
For the guilt be upon you
For judgment is near
As God is our witness
He will judge you for the innocent you tormented
For the pure you disgraced
For the lives you disposed of
And blackened the skies

Tremble earth tremble
For by evil and hate you lived
By bigotry and destruction
Were your deeds
You were vultures in human disguise
For blood was your drink
And flesh was your food
For you bathed in filth
And polluted the universe
For your disrupting nature
And everything in it
For your destroying the world

Tremble earth tremble
We are the testimonial accusers
The Jewish Holocaust survivors
Escaped from the flaming fires
And chilled cold ashes
With our tormented souls
And tortured bodies
From the death camps
To testify against your crimes
We and our shadows
Will forever hunt you
For justice is calling
For truth to prevail
Never forget, never fail
Remember, remember, remember.

The memories of the Holocaust are carved in my mind, my heart and my soul. It is an experience that inscribed itself in the deepest parts of me. As a young, carefree and happy girl in Poland before the War, I never could have imaged what life would have in store for me, nor could I have ever imagined spending my teenage years in a life or death struggle to survive a nightmare. I am often asked *how* I survived the daily horror, torture and terror of those years. I don't know *how* I survived. There is no logical explanation. Mother was a hero throughout it all and she was much of the reason. Etka too. Also, my faith in God remained unshaken, guiding me, giving me hope, and staying with me through everything. Often, I ask myself, "*How?*" because, seeing what I saw, living what I lived, my survival is very much a miracle. Still, the more difficult question I ask myself is, "Why me?" To this, I also have no answer. I am alive, and have tried to do my best to write down my experience good and bad.

Sometimes, when I'm asked about my experience of the Holocaust, I will tell people that the Holocaust was an individual event *and* a collective happening – it happened to me and I saw it through my eyes, felt it uniquely in my bones, and it also happened to everybody. We all shared the same pain, torture, terror, deprivation, and suffering even though each person experienced it differently, saw it through their own eyes and felt it in their own way. This book is one individual's witness to that collective experience.

Rule

Who is the wise man
And who is the fool
They out battle each other
To win and to rule

Who be the ruler
And who be the slave
Who will rule justly
And who will enslave

Chapter 1

I was born in Łódź, Poland on December 24, 1925, the second child to David and Cyporah Getler. They named me Masha. I was just a few months from my fourteenth birthday on that fateful day in 1939 when the Nazi army marched into Łódź, a large, industrial city with a sizeable population. Roughly a week earlier, around the time of the German invasion of Poland on September 1, Father had escaped with some friends and relatives over the border to Russian-occupied Baranowicz. It was the last time any of us saw him and the first sign of things to come. Icek, my younger brother, was especially heartbroken to see Father go. Following Father's escape and before being forced into the ghetto, we received one final communication from him: a package containing Passover matzos, a photograph, and a letter telling us how much he missed us and that he was okay. He would wait eagerly for our arrival.

The day Father left was deeply sorrowful, filled with earnest wishes for a safe journey, hope for a quick end to the war, and plenty of hugs and tears. At the time, promises were made and we all looked forward to a fantastic, joyous reuniting. We were still laboring under the impression that this would be like any other war. Still suffering the illusion of predictability and continuity of daily life.

After Father left, and in the days following the German invasion, Mother had enlisted a guide to help the rest of us escape across the border to Baranowicz to be with him. The guide had special knowledge of how to get out of the city. He had access to a clandestine network and assured us he could prepare the safest path for travel. He used to visit our modest second-story apartment each evening with information or instructions on when and where to meet and how best the escape could happen.

Mother had prepared us with satchels packed and ready, telling us that we might have to leave at a moment's notice. But each night the guide returned with worse news. The war was getting worse for Poland and the atmosphere on the streets was tense. It quickly became less and less safe to try to cross out of the city and even harder to get over the border. Besides the coming army, one main obstacle was that Anti-Semitism had grown rampant among the local ethnic Germans and Nazi sympathizers in the native Polish population. Traveling freely and openly was difficult and dangerous. With the passing of just a few days, the German Army and SS personnel swarmed Łódź. The borders were closed and the guide stopped coming to our apartment. By September 23, 1939 Warsaw, and all of Poland with it, fell to the Germans. There would be no escape anymore, no joyous reunion with Father.

As cities go, Łódź before the Nazi takeover had had a lively pulse and energy. It was a viable center of culture and industry with a bustling economy and thriving, long-standing Jewish population. The city always attracted new residents who came seeking jobs among the many factories. Anti-Semitism was certainly a reality but it never infringed as dramatically on our lives as it did in the weeks leading up to and just after the German invasion. It was shocking to see the hatred so plainly and openly expressed. I was not familiar with such overt hostility, nor did I know anything about wars or invasions beyond what was taught in history books or what Mother and Father had told us about the previous war. I knew even less about the evil and harm individual human beings were capable of doing to each other.

Our family lived on Kilinskiego Street. It was a large street, always abuzz with people and activity. At night you could see vibrant crowds of young adults and teenagers on the streets walking home from gymnasium or going to one of their organization meetings for the young Zionists or some other group. But, practically overnight, the streets quieted. The liveliness and crowds disappeared. Not even the Polish people felt comfortable walking freely anymore. Everybody disappeared into his or her homes, afraid and hiding. They didn't come out for years after. With overwhelming force and intimidation, the SS took complete control of public life. A pallor of fear fell quickly over everything. Gradually the city I adored and always called my home became a stranger. The familiar old buildings, courtyards, alleyways, lines of storefronts and workshops all grew motionless and silent. Gone was our life of warmth, security, and ease. Only memories remained.

I have especially fond memories of our family life before the war. Mother and Father had a wonderful relationship. They cared sincerely for each other, for us children, and for all of our uncles and aunts and their children. Mother, normally the taskmaster, could relax around Father who loved to spoil her and, in doing so, could bring out the joyful child in her. Mother's name was Cyporah. We called her "Mamusia" or "Mami" in Polish. Father called her Cypela, or more affectionately in Yiddish, Cypela *mayn feygele*, Cypela *my bird*.

"How are you children? Where's Cypela mayn feygele?" he would ask as he came through the door in the evening. Then he'd kiss my older sister Etka, brother Icek, and me on the forehead and go find Mother in the kitchen singing or humming a song as she finished cooking.

We called Father "Tatuś" in Polish, or "Tati." He was a patient man of impeccable integrity. He was very easy to talk to and always made time for people who wanted to speak to him or who sought his counsel. He loved people and people loved him. He was a good husband and attentive family man—a compassionate, loving father. He was only thirty-six in September of 1939.

Father's name was David Getler. He was twenty when he and Mother married. She was sixteen. He came from a pious and loving Jewish family who lived in Yendziv, Poland a town not too far from Łódź. Father didn't say too much about his childhood or his background. His parents died when he was young, long before I was born. But I was still curious. "What were your parents like," I once asked him.

Sitting in his armchair in the hazy light that streamed in through our apartment windows, he answered, "If they were alive, they would have loved you as much as I do." He went on to tell me that they were terrific parents, unpresuming people of meager means who loved their children dearly. I was nine or ten years old at the time and that's all I ever learned of Father's history.

Father had a brother named Asher who resided in Yendziv where he owned a business, and a sister named Fradla whose husband, Heskel, owned the import/export textile business where Father worked as a manager. Fradla and Heskel were hard working, generous and kind people. Asher was a conscientious and pleasant person. He used to come to Łódź to purchase raw materials and other goods from Uncle

3

Heskel. He would stay at Aunt Fradla's for a day, visit us for a meal, and then go back home on the train to Yendziv.

Mother was the third of five children—two sons and three daughters. Her parents had also died when she was young. Her extended family along with her eldest sister, Feigi Leah, supported the children until they were all old enough to marry or to live on their own. One day, when my brother and sister and I had just come home from school, Etka asked about our grandparents. Mother said plainly, "When I was about eleven years old, your *Dziadek,* grandfather, came down with the flu and died and so did your *Babcia,* grandmother. They died within one week of each other."

She continued to tell the story of how her mother's death happened. One morning, her mother called all of the children into the room and asked them to sit near. Sensing something important, Mother and her siblings were all ears, anxiously awaiting her words. She sat up and said how much she loved them but that the time had come for her to go and that she would be leaving them shortly.

Frightened, the children broke into tears. "What is going to happen to us?" they asked. "Father is gone. Now you are leaving too. We will be all alone."

In a weak, soft voice, she replied, "Don't worry. Our family will do their best to take care of you. Remember to take care of each other. God will always be with you. Be good and be brave. I love you all very much." With that, she died.

Mother wasn't a woman who minced words or engaged in extended discussions about unimportant things. Somewhat of an enigma, she was rugged and soft at the same time. She had a tough face with happy eyes, round, high cheekbones and beautiful black wavy hair. Her toughness made her resilient against the harshest that life could throw at her. She always faced crisis with tireless, sharp presence of mind and endurance of spirit.

She got her strength from a uniquely clear vision of the present, an unwavering aversion to wallowing in the past, and a secure faith that the future would be okay. Her disposition was generally jovial, even if she was somewhat forthright and strong-willed. Within our family, she was the strict disciplinarian. If we wanted something, we first tried our luck with Father because we knew Mother would surely say "No."

4

Still, we tried to get away with things, to test, as children are apt to do, how far we could go with her pragmatic patience. But she had a sixth sense for what we were up to and a cunning way of keeping us in line, of stopping us before we started, sometimes with just a well-directed stare.

She was the clear ruler of the roost, guiding and keeping order with love and attention. Her word was cast in stone and her directions were always to be obeyed. But despite this, she wasn't really a harsh woman. She never punished us aggressively. Instead, in righting our wrongs she was more concerned that we learned from our mistakes so that we could understand that the important thing was to move forward, beyond them. Moving forward was her primary way of being. Her primary purpose was to comfort, to protect, to provide, to care for and to love. It was a simple formula that helped her create a happy home environment and that later, more than once, also saved my life. She was just thirty-two in 1939 when our world changed forever.

Mother's oldest brother was named Mayer. Uncle Mayer and his wife had two daughters who were close in age to myself. Their names were Chana and Ethel. Next to Mayer was Feigi Leah. Feigi Leah was married and lived with her husband in Ostrowiec. Then came Mother, my favorite aunt, Aunt Mania, and finally the youngest, Uncle Hershel. Uncle Hershel with his wife and young children, and also Father's sister, Fradla, would end up confined in the Łódź ghetto with us.

Many years before the war, Uncle Mayer's wife had died and he moved from Ostrowiec to Łódź with Ethel, his youngest daughter. His eldest daughter, Chana, a very stable and mature girl, already had a job and so stayed in Ostrowiec with Aunt Feigi Leah. Ethel lived with us because it was easier for Uncle Mayer. She was like another sister and we were very close. In 1938, Uncle Mayer himself became very sick and was admitted to the hospital. We visited him often but his health deteriorated rapidly. The prognosis was not good. Soon Chana also came to Łódź to stay with us and to be with her ailing father.

One night, while Uncle Mayer was in the hospital, I was awakened by a dream. Scared, I screamed. My scream alarmed and woke everyone in the house. Mother came running into my room and asked what was wrong. I told her that I'd seen the door between the kitchen and the hallway swing wide open and Uncle Mayer come walking in

5

through it. Mother knew that the kitchen door was kept strictly closed at night to keep as much heat in the house as possible. Mother sat at my bedside and quietly told me not to worry about it and to go back to sleep. But I couldn't fall asleep. Neither could she apparently. A few moments after she left our room, I heard her walk down the hall and pull the kitchen door tightly shut.

In the morning I spied Mother and Father fully dressed, tiptoeing noiselessly out of the house. Later, they told us they had taken a bus and gone to the hospital to check on Uncle Mayer. When they arrived, they were told that he had passed away at midnight, about the same time I had awakened from my dream.

Our family took in Chana and Ethel. Ethel was just one or two years younger than me – about twelve years old. Like a younger sister, she endearingly copied and followed everything Etka and I would do. She was a sweet girl, a loyal friend, and a good listener. Chana was a few years older than me and was a dependable, responsible girl. It wasn't long after their Father died that the Germans would attack Łódź, and not long after that the we would see Chana for the last time.

Aunt Mania, Mother's youngest sister, was my favorite aunt. Closest to our family, she too lived with us for many years. Fun and full of life, Mania had the most wonderful, full smile of perfect, lustrous teeth and bright dimples. She was slender and tall, with thick, dark-brown hair, sparkling green eyes and a porcelain complexion. She was beautiful, and I revered her beauty.

Mania's beauty helped her attract many suitors, and she had no problem finding boyfriends. Once upon a time she was in love with a young man named Moshe. They were mad for each other and spent countless hours together. To us, it was a storybook romance and we thought surely it would end in a happy engagement and long, happy lives as husband and wife. But the relationship didn't work out. Mania was stubborn as well as beautiful, and her mind, when made up, was not easily changed. At one point, she simply and rather abruptly decided that it was time to get married. Moshe, however, wanted to wait. He wasn't financially prepared. He wanted to have money to rent an apartment and to buy furniture and other necessities. He tried to convince Mania to be patient, but his attempts were futile. Mania said that she would be an old maid by the time he was ready and that if Moshe weren't ready at that point, then he never would be. So they parted. I could see that he was heartbroken. We liked Moshe and we were all a little saddened.

A couple of years before the war broke out, Mania met another young man who was more mature and more established than Moshe. He had been a decorated and ranked soldier in the Polish army, had a respectable reputation, and made a good living. Not long after meeting her, he proposed. She accepted and they got married. In a year's time, they had their first and only son, an angelic little boy who became their every joy. But because of her husband's experience in the army, when the Germans marched into Łódź, Mania and her husband were taken. They were on a list of "political prisoners," people who could be a threat to the Nazis.

Chapter 2

My childhood in Łódź was generally agreeable, peaceful and normal. Our home was happy and comfortable, our days, harmonious. Though we weren't really wealthy, our lives were rich and very full. My sister, Etka, was born two years before me–Mother and Father had her shortly after they were married. Icek, my younger brother, was born three years after me. Of the three of us, Etka looked most like Mother. She was an energetic child, always curious and into some kind of athletic or social activity. She did well in school and was extremely popular; she liked people and people liked her. She was sixteen years old when the Germans occupied Łódź.

Icek was as much like our father as any boy could be like his father– similarly modest, quiet and calm. He only spoke when he had to or when he felt like he had something necessary to say. Icek was witty and curious and fun to be around. As young children, we used to go to the park together, hold onto each other's hands and laugh. He was a good listener and unusually supportive and caring for such a young boy. Hardly a whisper of complaint ever escaped his lips, even when the unending hunger took hold.

Icek's eyes were exceedingly blue, bluer than mine. They gave him a very intense yet tranquil look. His gaze seemed inward and it made him look like there was always something terribly complex on his mind. He was tall and strong for his age and looked much older than his eleven years. Because of this, Icek was able to escape the systematic deportations of children from the ghetto.

Etka, Icek and I kept very busy with school, chores, and family and friends. Icek had a lot of energy and was always active, playing ball or doing something else on the street outside with the other boys his age. He also went to school and to cheder to study Hebrew, prayers, and other religious things. Etka was athletic and sociable and spent much of her time at the community center. I preferred to spend my free time visiting with friends and talking. I would go to my best friend Ala's house and have long, involved conversations about whatever was happening in our immediate lives. What I loved to do more, though, was to read. I would read the most beautiful poetry. And sometimes I would write just for the sake of writing. It was something that was deep within me.

We lived in a simple, second-floor apartment. It had three rooms, a kitchen, a sitting area and a place to eat. It wasn't big, but it was sufficient for our needs, hospitable to guests, and welcoming to family. Our days were largely uneventful and filled with the common concerns of everyday family life. On weekdays, Father would wake up first and leave the house early for work. Then Mother would come into the room that Etka and I shared and wake us up. We'd dress groggily, have a small bite to eat and shuffle out the door to school.

We had access to both religious education and secular public education in our city. Etka and I went to one of the secular Jewish public schools. It was an all-girl school. I remember the school being impeccably clean. The windows never had smudges, there was no dust anywhere, and the floors were so pristine that you could eat off of them. For some reason this was of the highest importance to the school administrators. Every morning, before classes we did gymnastics and said a little prayer. It wasn't a denominational prayer, just a small "We thank God for everything around us" kind of prayer.

We took our studies pretty seriously. The class work consisted of the usual subjects: geography, history, mathematics, Polish, poetry. Once or twice a week we had to take a sewing class. We learned different kinds of stitching and patterns. I wasn't very good and didn't like it. I never finished my projects but it didn't matter because Etka would finish them for me. After school some of the boys would go to Shul to study Torah and Talmud. At the time, it wasn't common for girls to go to Shul. Most didn't and Etka and I were no exception.

When I was about six or seven years old, classmates, friends and even my sister and brother began to call me "Marysia." I had blue eyes and light-colored, almost blonde hair. People didn't believe that I was Jewish. On the street, strangers would stop to touch my hair or inspect my face, saying, "I don't believe it, this child cannot be Jewish!" My appearance though, did not help to make me any less afraid or change my fate as a Jewish person under Nazi brutality.

When we got home in the afternoon, we would excitedly recount our day to Mother who would listen closely while remaining busy with some household task. We told her what happened at school that day and what we liked or disliked about it. Sometimes we complained or made an argument to which she was sure to play devil's advocate just to challenge our perspective. Sometimes though, she would refuse to take a side at all because she didn't like to hear gossip and wanted to teach us not to do it.

These afternoons were spent doing chores or homework and waiting for Father to come home. Often he would arrive tired but was always in good spirits and delighted to see his family. "How's my Cypela? How was your day?" he'd ask Mother.

Mother would answer, "Fine. How was yours?"

"It went well. I'm happy to be home," he'd say smiling, turning to us and adding ironically, "You all weren't waiting for me, were you?"

Then he would sit down in an armchair or at the dining table, prompting us to burst out enthusiastically, sometimes all at once, shouting whatever came to our minds, barraging him with questions or *kvetching* about something.

He would respond kindly, "Okay. Let's see what's bothering you, but first let's sit down and have the meal that Mother has prepared for us. We will talk afterwards." This quieted us instantly, and as the sun cast long orange shadows across the living room, we gathered at the table to enjoy our meal. After the meal, we forgot all about whatever it was that was bothering us, settled down to read or play, and then drifted off to sleep.

The summers in Łódź could get unbearably hot. Mother coped poorly with the heat. It made the pollution from all the factory smokestacks hang thick in the heavy, sticky air. Luckily, as was common with many Łódź citizens, we could escape to the fresher air of the countryside. Having so many people travel outside the city made the summers there lively and fun. Some people owned houses, others would rent. Some stayed for the entire summer, others came for a few weeks or just a few days.

Aunt Fradla and Uncle Heskel owned a villa in Adamowek where they spent their summers with their children. It was only about an hour away from Łódź by bus. When Etka, Icek and I were very young, Father used to take us to Aunt Fradla's villa. Later, when we grew older and when Father could afford it, he rented us a place of our own either in Adamowek or Helenowek.

The countryside was a wonderful, picturesque escape. There were large swaths of open, grassy fields dotted with small farms and forests of tall, skinny trees with streams running through them. I remember stepping high through the fields of tall grass with Icek on our way to play at the streamside, or walking the long, hilly dirt-roads to meet Mother or Father at the bus station. There were wild berries everywhere – raspberries, blueberries, blackberries. My favorites were the blueberries. We would pick bushels of them with Mother who would take them back home to Łódź and bake all kinds of delicious pastries. There was a river where everybody used to gather to swim and cool off. During the evening, groups of teenagers would bring different kinds of musical instruments to a veranda at the river's edge. They would play music, sing and dance long into the night. Occasionally, Aunt Mania would come to the countryside with us and take us to be with the teenagers when they played. She and Moshe were friendly with them. Father had to work in the summers so he spent only the weekends or just Sunday with us. He'd finish work and observe *Shabbat* and then come out on the first bus Sunday morning and go home late Sunday night in order to get back to work the next morning. When the summers ended, we returned to the city, suntanned, rested, and ready for school and another cold winter.

Before the invasion, the Jewish community in Łódź had been immense – roughly 230,000, about one-third the population of the entire city. Next to Warsaw, it was the second largest Jewish community in Poland. For the most part, we lived peacefully and integrated well with the Polish people and the ethnic Germans, the *Volksdeutchen*, living in Łódź. We maintained our Jewish identity but considered ourselves Polish as well as Jewish. In fact, many Jewish people had roots going back generations in the area and remained fervently nationalistic to Poland. But even with our singular shared Jewish heritage, there were vast differences among groups within the Jewish population. Lots of different ideologies and ways of thinking shaped the community. There were religious and secular differences, differences between Zionist and non-Zionist groups, and differences between socialist, communist and capitalist.

All of the Zionist organizations shared the common aim of wanting to find a way to settle in *Eretz Israel*. They each had different ideas about how to go about doing this. Some people in the community cared about the Zionist ideas and some people didn't. Some were simply happy where they lived and didn't want to leave. Others were patriotic and dedicated to Poland and couldn't imagine leaving. Certain Zionists did actually emigrate as *Halutzim*, "pioneers," to *Eretz Israel* before the war. My great Aunt Sarah's son was one of them. He was passionate about settlement and, despite the harshness and emptiness of the land, when he was old enough, emigrated there. My aunt sold half her building to support him in his dream of being a pioneer. Later, he was stricken with Malaria and died.

There were economic differences among the Jewish people. From wealthy to middle to working class to poor beggars, all social classes and walks of life were present in the city. Industrialists, doctors, lawyers, small business owners, teachers, tailors, homemakers, shoemakers, bakers, barbers, and countless other professions counted Jewish people among their ranks. Wealth and poverty walked peacefully side by side on the streets of Łódź.

There was also a varied and fertile cultural and civic aspect to life in Łódź. There were many journalists, intellectuals, writers, musicians, poets, artists, humorists, and architects who built the most stunningly beautiful synagogues. There were Jewish theaters and newspapers and other publications. Civic life was of the utmost importance. We took pride in our community and in our families. We valued high morals and ethics; the imprint of the Torah, its laws and teachings were written in our actions, in our making. We went about our days with vigor, joy and commitment. Our contributions could be seen in every field, industry and endeavor.

The Nazis swept this away with the barrels of their guns and their hatred. It was part of their plan of racial purification to strip us of our Jewish identity, to shatter our world and lay waste to our humanity before killing us. From their first marching steps onto our streets, they harassed, beat, shot, and tortured us. They would use fists, guns, dogs, ghettos, gas chambers, disease, starvation, and violence of all kinds to wreak their destruction. In what seemed like the blink of an eye, our normal, pleasant existence, our entire world got turned on its head, our hopes and dreams turned to nightmares.

The Nazis brought on a time of total darkness. No sun, no moon, no stars, no light. Everywhere we turned there was a different Nazi snare. They obliterated the former peace and happiness of life in Łódź. Everywhere, there was random violence. Every day we felt that our world was coming to an end. The law of the Nazis was a law of ruination. But there is a higher law to the order of the universe, and I believe we only survived the daily horror and shock of Nazi violence because this law dictates one must ultimately transmit the utmost good to others. Life is a gift to be lived to its fullest. This is God's will. And God's will transcends man's will. To turn against it is to violate God's given law. Evil is not part of the nature of God's will. It's a result of our actions, created by unnatural human behavior. I believe that someday by virtue of free will, we will follow God's law of doing the utmost good, and evil will be a thing of the past.

Chapter 3

One day, a year before the invasion, Etka came home very excited. She told me that she joined a Zionist organization called Betar. Etka was young, energetic and full of ideals at the time. She wasn't a Zionist nor was she that political, but many of her friends belonged to Betar and she had a good time at their gatherings. She went to their meetings because it was a place to get together socially, to dance and sing and have fun with people her own age.

The afternoon prior to one particular Betar gathering, she came home from school very excited. She had heard that a special speaker was going to be at the meeting to talk at length about Eretz Israel and to dispense important information for people interested in becoming *Halutzim*, pioneers. She was filled with the energy and the excitement of being part of that group and said that an opportunity like this did not come very often. She was determined to be there. But Mother didn't want her to go. Mother wasn't feeling well and needed Etka to do some things around the house so that she could rest. "I want you to stay home until Father gets back from work," she told Etka, "then you can go." Etka's excitement quickly deflated.

Mother's answer stung, but Etka couldn't wait and wasn't going to obey Mother. As soon as she noticed Mother fall asleep, she asked me to cover for her by helping out with the chores she was supposed to do. She told me that she would be back soon and not to worry. I agreed and she exited in a hurry. She had been gone only about half an hour before returning. It was sooner than I expected, so I asked what happened, what the speaker had to say. But Etka didn't want to talk and brushed me off.

"Everything was fine. I'm too tired to talk about it now," she said. "I'm going to go lie down and catch up on some reading for school."

She was oddly sensitive so I didn't push. She disappeared into the bedroom.

The following morning, as Etka and I were walking to school I noticed she had a limp. She said it was nothing much, she had just bumped into something. The morning of the next day though, she was in so much pain that she couldn't get out of bed. Mother went into our room and wanted to know what was wrong. Etka was going to be late for school if she didn't hurry.

Etka struggled to stand up and I could see the pain on her face as her feet hit the floor. She just couldn't stand up no matter how hard she tried, nor could she hide from Mother whatever was wrong. Etka sat on the edge of her bed with her bare feet resting gingerly on the tile floor. Mother's eyes zeroed in on Etka's ankles. One of them was horribly bruised, red, and swollen. Mother immediately demanded to know what happened and how. Etka was quiet a moment, then burst into tears and confessed that she had gone to the Betar meeting in spite of being told not to. She paused and waited for punishment or rebuke, but Mother said nothing. Etka continued to describe how at the meeting many people were milling about, waiting for the speaker to arrive. There were heavy benches for the audience, but not much space to maneuver between the benches and the bodies in the crowd. Etka said she'd moved to sit down when the bench somehow turned over and landed right on her foot, smashing it. It was so painful that she couldn't stay at the meeting. Some concerned friends helped her get home.

Mother nodded and listened intently as Etka spoke. She wasn't angry but was upset that Etka hadn't told her. She took Etka right away to see a doctor. The doctor looked at her foot and ankle and diagnosed a fracture. He gave her a brace to hold the ankle in place and instructed her to keep the foot elevated. She was told not to walk on it too much until she came back in a few weeks and was given the all clear.

The few weeks passed but the ankle worsened. It grew more swollen and bruised, and now seemed completely crooked and out of joint. She went back to the doctor. He examined her, took an x-ray, and then sent her directly to the hospital that had a special ward for bone corrections. The hospital had a good reputation and was known for bringing in

15

foreign doctors to perform special surgeries. But it was on the outskirts of the city and too far to walk so we had to take the tramway to get there. Once there, another doctor examined Etka and said she needed surgery immediately. The ankle had healed badly and needed to be corrected. Luckily, there was a very good American doctor on site who waited for the swelling to decrease and then operated successfully. Etka stayed in the hospital for a few weeks, and while she was there we visited her everyday. It wasn't a long walk to and from the tramway stops, but it was a long enough walk that I could tell something in the city's atmosphere was changing. Everyday the city was growing slightly more hostile.

One night, it was getting late and we had to leave Etka by herself in the hospital. Etka wanted badly to go home with us, but she wasn't cleared yet to walk. We hugged and kissed, said some comforting words and parted. Outside on the street that evening, the air felt particularly strange–heavy and oppressive. People didn't want to look at us. They ignored us or did the opposite and stared outright. For a while, anti-Semitism had been seeming to take hold, but had yet to become open and overt. Now though, as we passed the side of a building, we saw it plainly and clearly written in profane, messy graffiti: "Jews get out of our country! Go back to Palestine," and "We will get rid of you one way or another!"

Things in Poland soon grew out of control. News of stone throwing and beatings became more common. There were regular outbreaks of violence, mostly against men, in different parts of the city. There were also reports of awful pogroms in smaller Polish towns. When walking to the tramway stop to visit Etka, we were scared. But mother wouldn't show it. She held my hand firmly and we marched to where we had to go. We visited Etka religiously, passing through those increasingly dangerous streets until she was discharged with a clean bill of health and an order to go easy on the ankle.

Just before the invasion, there was terrible confusion in the Jewish community. People began fleeing in all directions–from Łódź to Warsaw, from Warsaw back to Łódź and other places based on where they thought they would be safest. When one place was bombed out, people would flee and go to another. When another place was bombed, they would leave there too. We all understood that the German Army was on an unstoppable march. And we didn't hold out much hope for the embattled Polish Army. We knew that if the Germans decided to take Poland, that Poland would likely be defeated. If that happened, it would only be a matter of time before they would come marching down our own Kilinskiego Street. Still, there were many unanswered questions. Where would we go? Why? What would or could they possibly do to us?

After a certain point, we had heard enough rumors of the Jews in Germany being displaced from their homes, read enough newspaper reports of Hitler spewing his madness against Jews that we had to make a choice. Stay in our home and risk the same fate or escape to and unknown, yet safer place? We decided to escape. Our family and our neighbors got together to discuss the situation and come up with the best plan for leaving.

With the German invasion of Poland on September 1, our urgency increased. The adults convened and decided not to wait any longer. The Polish Army was being overtaken and pushed back into retreat. The German army would certainly enter the city shortly and clamp down on the local population. Escape would then likely be difficult if not impossible. A plan, a day and a destination were chosen. In two evenings we were to gather in our building and set out in small groups at times not far apart from each other. Our destination was Baranowicz, a town over the border in Russian territory.

The day of departure came and people were streaming in and out of our apartment. Etka, Ethel, Icek and I stayed together in our living room. We were waiting quietly for instructions from the adults. It was a tense time. People made the final preparations and prepared a hasty goodbye to their homes. I looked over at Mother and saw that she was terribly worried about something. She was speaking earnestly about something to Father who seemed to be growing frustrated with whatever she was saying. What was going on was that Aunt Mania, her husband and their baby boy hadn't shown up to join us yet. Mother wanted to go to Mania's apartment to see what was happening and Father didn't want her to go. Finally Chana resolved the issue by volunteering to go instead of Mother. Father reluctantly agreed.

Chana left the apartment and ventured over to Aunt Mania's. As we waited for her return, the concern grew in mother's face again. She paced back and forth near the window. She pulled the curtain aside every now and then, hoping to see Chana arriving with Mania, her husband and the baby. But they never appeared and it was taking too long. Aunt Mania did not live that far away. Chana should have returned with them or at least with some news. Finally, Mother decided to find out for herself what was going on.

When she arrived at Aunt Mania's, she found Mania inconsolably distressed. Her baby was terribly ill with a high fever. Mother pleaded with her, but Mania said she wouldn't travel with the baby in that condition. She told mother and Chana that they should go ahead. She said that she, her husband and the baby would join us later. Mother didn't like the idea that Mania would be delayed or that she could be traveling alone with an infant. But Chana offered to stay behind to help. Reluctantly and with a heavy heart, Mother agreed to leave her youngest sister and her niece and came back to our apartment.

On the way home, she made up her mind that she would stay behind with us children in Łódź to wait for Mania's baby to be well enough to travel. She told Father of her decision. He became uncharacteristically agitated. He wanted our family to stay together but the pressure to leave was mounting. It was getting late. The neighbors were eager to get moving and wanted to know what the delay was. Mother assured Father that it would only be a few days before Mania's baby would be well enough to make the journey. In the meantime, she told him he could go on ahead and find a place for us to live in Baranowicz. She finally convinced him that women and children would be much safer than men and that he must go for that reason. The decision was made that he would go on ahead without us.

As he walked out to join the group of neighbors waiting on the street, we ran to him with tears in our eyes and bowed our heads so he could kiss the top of our foreheads like he usually did. But instead, he hugged each of us tightly and kissed us. He told us to take good care of Mother and not to worry since we wouldn't be apart for long. Then he hugged and kissed Mother and said goodbye. It was difficult for us to see him go. We all had tears in our eyes, including him.

In the days that followed, Mother went often to look in on Chana, Aunt Mania and the baby. The baby wasn't getting better. Meanwhile, the sounds of the German Army on the attack approached our city. Air raid sirens went off continually and the bombs and mortar explosions grew closer until they were practically on top of us. Mother was getting terribly anxious and wanted to convince Aunt Mania that we had to go, that the baby would have to be okay to travel. She went again to Aunt Mania's, this time ready to demand that her sister come with us to escape. But when Mother arrived, she found the door to Aunt Mania's apartment closed and locked with a double lock. Her heart jumped. She tried to open the door and then started knocking loudly until an old man who lived in the apartment next door peeked his head out. He had always been a nice man, smiling and saying hello when we passed. He waved Mother over to his door and told her that the German Gestapo had been to Mania's apartment. They had a list. Aunt Mania's and her husband's names were on it. They forced not only Aunt Mania and her husband, but also the baby and Chana to go with them. That was the last we heard or saw of them. We never found out where they were taken. Early the next morning, the German Army entered Łódź.

Chapter 4

The Germans were extraordinarily organized and well prepared for their entry into Łódź. The lists that the Gestapo arrived with, the ones that had Aunt Mania's and her husband's names, were seemingly compiled ahead of time, plans for the removal of the people on the lists laid out accordingly. The lists were remarkably complete. The Gestapo knew where people lived and who owned what property or factory or workshop. Though we never knew for sure, we figured that they either had spies in the city, made deals with the local Polish government, or had help from the sympathetic Polish and German people to create these lists. Either way, by the time September 8 came, the Germans had complete control and thorough knowledge of the community. Mother, Etka, Ethel, Icek and I still hoped that an opportunity would arise for us to get out, but now we were trapped.

The Germans wasted no time in bringing down decree after decree and order after order on the Jews in the city. First it was the yellow armbands. They called it "Jewish yellow." Then the curfews, then the yellow signs over Jewish businesses and in shop windows that read "Jüde." Then the armbands were replaced with the Star of David that had to be sewn onto your outer clothing, which mother and Etka had to do with whatever cloth was lying around the house.

Each day the situation grew worse for the Jewish community. More and more Jews were thrown out of their homes, their possessions ending up in piles in the middle of the streets for the German trucks and wagons to come haul off to who knew where. Armoires, sideboards, mirrors, chandeliers, carpets, tables and chairs stood like a haphazard and awkward still life of tangled branches and roots of trees. All valuables had to be surrendered: jewelry, gold, silver, złoty or currency of any kind. Failure to surrender meant you could be beaten, shot, deported or become the victim of whatever struck the sadistic fancy of a particular SS person or Nazi soldier enforcing an order. For the most part, people did what they were forced to do. Yet obeying the German orders never guaranteed our safety. Disobeying, however, surely guaranteed retribution.

The streets eventually became a prison where the German guards were free to do to you as they pleased. Jews were randomly plucked off the street and forced to clean toilets, to wash windows and floors, to bow or kneel in deference or dance around foolishly. Whatever indignity could be conjured up for their perverse amusement, some Nazi soldier or Gestapo would find a way to enact it on a Jewish person. Most of the time it was within sight of the local Poles and *Volksdeutsche*–our fellow countrymen. Often it was with their help. We were powerless to stop the onslaught of hatred and violence.

The laws changed so often that it became impossible to keep up with what was defined as a crime and what wasn't. Everything seemed like a crime, and all crimes seemed punishable by immediate imprisonment or death. We became paranoid and frozen. Just existing in the line of sight of an SS man was a precarious prospect. Whatever customs and laws of civility, reason and rationality that had been in place previously were killed, made into ghosts. What took their place was the law of brutality, cruelty, and irrationality.

Economic and cultural life came to a tragic standstill. Factories closed and people lost their jobs. Severe limitations on how much złoty Jewish people could have in the bank or at home were levied. Jews were forbidden to walk on certain streets or ride buses or the tramway. Jewish shops were forced to sell only Jewish goods to Jewish people or were shut down completely. Most of them became unprofitable and folded. During Rosh Hashanah that year, the Germans forced the stores open and the synagogues closed. The synagogues remained closed and were quickly vandalized, set on fire, or dynamited. World-famous, magnificent synagogues, like the ones on Wolborska Street or Aleya Kosciusko, were torched or blown up. There was no regard for the sanctity or the history of those beautiful buildings. The streets shook as the explosions of dynamite went off all over the city. The place where we were born, the place of love, goodness, and warmth was destroyed in those blasts, disappearing in shards of stone, dust and smoke.

Eventually any semblance of human or humane treatment by the occupying force vanished. In the beginning, for example, we could still walk the streets somewhat freely. Later, we could only walk the streets during the day, never at night. Still later, we could only walk the streets a couple of hours a day. Finally, we couldn't walk the streets at all if the streets were outside the ghetto. We tried our best to maintain a sense of normalcy despite the increasing oppression. At first, we kept going to school but after just two or three weeks school was forbidden to us. To stay busy, despite our anxiety, Ethel, Icek and I would go to our friends' houses to play and talk, certain always to come home before the curfew.

I took a walk one day probably at the beginning of 1940 to visit my Aunt Fradla. Her husband, Uncle Heskel, had passed away just before the war. Aunt Fradla and her two children lived in a huge apartment in a building that she owned. She was delighted to see me. She wanted to know as much as possible about the rest of the family and if we had heard from Father. I told her that we had. A few days earlier we had received a letter and a package from him. The package included a photo of him and some matzos he baked for us. In the letter, he wrote that he hoped we would receive them in time for Passover. He also wrote that he was doing fine, that he was worried about us, loved and missed us but that we shouldn't worry about him. He was still in Baranowicz and would wait there until we could be together again. I was so happy to have heard from him that I carried the letter around with me like a little treasure. I showed Aunt Fradla the letter and she read it. She was relieved to have news from him and, knowing that Father wasn't much of a baker, laughed when she read about the matzos.

She asked me to stay and have lunch. We went into the kitchen and began preparing it when, suddenly, there was a booming knock at the door. Normally before any knock, the bell from the downstairs entrance would ring to let us know somebody wanted to come into the building and come upstairs. But this had not happened. We knew something was wrong. Aunt Fradla and I stood silently, uneasily, listening as Zofia, Aunt Fradla's maid, went to the door and asked who was there.

"Open the door"– "*Machen es shnell*."–"Make it fast!" a voice yelled in German.

Before Zofia could have the latch completely undone, two uniformed German officers stormed in and burst past her. They ordered my aunt and me to stay in the kitchen while they "inspected" the home. We stayed frozen in place waiting to see what they wanted, what they would do, what they were "inspecting."

Both officers were only of average height but one was younger than the other. Their appearance was extremely neat and clean. Their uniforms were well pressed and they moved arrogantly, wooden and upright like they didn't want to wrinkle their uniforms. The elder officer looked into rooms while the young one stood in the kitchen doorway eyeing us. He removed his hat and began to brush lint from it, flicking pieces away like he was flicking away fleas. His strange, predatory smile frightened me.

The elder officer finally said, "This will do. You are ordered to vacate immediately. Take your family and leave. Do not touch or take anything from the house. If you do take something it will be considered theft."

The officers were going to take the apartment for themselves and their own families. If Aunt Fradla kept anything of real value or tried to remove furniture, she would be put in prison or killed. There was no time to gather things anyway. We were being instantly chased from everything we knew, and we had to scurry like hunted animals.

Zofia had the temerity to ask them if she could take a few things that belonged to her. She pleaded that she was only the Polish housekeeper and would like to keep her pictures, bedding, and other small personal belongings. The officers said that they would wait but that she should hurry.

Aunt Fradla was beside herself but couldn't say anything. She hurriedly shepherded me out the door. Frightened, I walked down the hall to the stairs and looked back just once. I saw the younger German officer peek his head out and watch me leave. It gave me a cold chill and I started running down the steps. As I reached the front door, the door that was to have remained locked and where people would ring to come up, I passed Aunt Fradla's janitor. I knew instantly that he was the one who let the officers in. He was an old man with a wisp of hair that always fell over his face. He seemed to shrug as if to say, "What could I do?"

Outside, the air was cool. Spring had not fully arrived and there was still a chill in the air. I stopped a moment, suddenly realizing I had been holding my breath. I exhaled and inhaled deeply and heard some shouting coming from the apartment above. Then the shouting stopped and an eerie quiet fell over the street. I started for home.

Not long after I'd exited, Aunt Fradla vacated her home and left her belongings and moved in with a tenant of hers. Later she would be deported to the ghetto in one of the regional deportation groups. From there, she would be sent with her two children to Auschwitz, where they were murdered. She was not alone in this fate. The Germans went block by block, house by house, building by building, commandeering people's homes, robbing them of their property. When the ghetto was finally created, every Jewish person, save those who already lived in the ghetto area before its designation as a ghetto, was effectively displaced. Nobody had a home anymore.

As I walked back to our apartment I tried to choke back the tears but I couldn't stop sobbing. I was consumed by what I had just witnessed. My aunt's dignity and self-worth were shattered like glass. Her life, her home, her possessions, whatever meant something to her was meaningless to them. How could this be? I looked up from staring at the ground as I walked and noticed that I had just passed the building on the corner where my Great Aunt Sarah lived. Memories of going to her house with Father flashed through my head.

Aunt Sarah was a widow in her fifties. Perpetually bubbly and pleasant, she lived in a large, well-appointed street-level apartment. The last time Father and I had visited her was in passing on our way home from doing errands. We stopped and rang the doorbell. She opened the door and welcomed us with the sunniest smile. She invited us in and asked us to stay and have lunch. I could smell the sweet aromas coming from the kitchen and very much wanted to eat but Father told her we couldn't stay. When we were ready to leave I looked down the hall and saw that two men had opened the door to the dining room. They were standing, waiting, looking in our direction. Behind them through the dining room door, I saw Aunt Sarah's long, wooden table and many people sitting around it having lunch. Aunt Sarah glanced back at the men, then excused herself into the kitchen and reemerged with two envelopes. She handed one to each of the men.

They took them with a smile and a nod then exited the house. Father then thanked Aunt Sarah for the meal invitation and promised to see her again at a later date. We hugged and kissed her and said goodbye.

Father held my hand as we started to walk home. I didn't know why we couldn't stay and eat. I thought maybe Aunt Sarah was having some kind of special celebration that we couldn't interrupt. I asked Father who those people were and what they were doing. He replied that the people at Aunt Sarah's were poor but respectable members of our community who needed help. I didn't know what he meant. He explained that they were too proud to ask for handouts, to beg, or to accept charity from anyone. He said that in our community there are wonderful people who secretly support and protect others from dishonor and that Aunt Sarah was one of them. She served meals to the poor once a week and gave them money to buy the things necessary to prepare *Shabbat* for their families. I thought that was great and noble and I admired her even more.

My thoughts wandered through memories like this until I finally arrived home. I had been rubbing my eyes red as I cried and walked. When mother saw me at the door, she knew that something terrible had happened. I burst into tears and told her everything about my visit with Aunt Fradla. She hugged me and brought me inside, not saying anything. Later that day, I glimpsed her staring silently out the window. She had a troubled countenance yet her thoughts looked like they were someplace else, perhaps with Father, perhaps with my Aunt Fradla or Aunt Mania or both. Had she been aware that I was watching, I probably wouldn't have seen that look on her face.

By the end of 1939 there would be no escaping anymore. It was forbidden for any Jewish person to travel outside one's town or place of residence. We did not yet know of the German's plans to confine us to a ghetto but we knew that they were expelling people from the city. We thought they were taking them to work camps but had no way of knowing for sure. In February 1940, we saw notices posted on walls and buildings and heard announcements on truck loudspeakers. All Jews were ordered to resettle in the northern part of the city immediately. The northern part of Łódź was called Baluty. It was an area mainly of Jews but plenty of Poles lived there as well. Baluty was a working-class neighborhood and most of the buildings were one or two room apartments where a single person or a couple with scant means might live comfortably.

Mother had resisted the order for forced registration that happened a few weeks earlier but this time she sensed that we must follow the order. If they could kick people out of their homes, if they could take over Aunt Fradla's by just going in and demanding that she leave, if they could take Aunt Mania and her family and make them disappear, surely they could remove us from our own modest apartment. So she went to the northern part of the city to seek out a place for us. She didn't want to wait until the last minute and suffer the indignity of being forcibly removed.

Many people did, however, resist the order to resettle in the ghetto, not wanting to give up their homes. It was an unbelievable and unreasonable request. Why would they make us leave our homes? What did that have to do with war? How could they move us to this place, the ghetto? These apartments weren't empty. People lived in them. But many of the Jews and some Poles in Baluty had fled before the German arrival. At first, for Poles and ethnic Germans living in Łódź, if you didn't have necessary business or a close relative, you were not to have any contact with this part of the city. Later, staying away from the ghetto became an official order. To make sure the area remained free of Poles and ethnic Germans, the SS spread the rumor that the ghetto was a hotbed of disease–typhus, dysentery, and others.

Mother found us a single room on the second floor of a small building that was on one side of a courtyard on 25 Zydowska Street. We were lucky to find the apartment we did. There was a double bed, a couch and a small table in the room. A young couple had occupied the place before us and the furniture was relatively new. Icek slept on the couch and the rest of us found space on the bed or on a mattress on the floor. There were two neighbors to either side of us, and two groups on the first floor. The bathroom was downstairs–three toilets for the entire building–and we ended up cooking whatever food we had on a small stove that the young couple had left behind.

The resettlement of Jews into the ghetto was supposed to have been efficient, organized and orderly. People were supposed to go at appointed times and in distinct groups. But there was too much disbelief. People were too despondent and confused. They would straggle along the streets, carrying their possessions in sacks or dragging things in wagons. People waited or hid, thinking maybe they could escape the resettlement. By the end of February, the resettlement wasn't taking place quickly or orderly enough for the German's satisfaction. Eventually a final decree was issued and anybody caught outside the ghetto was imprisoned, shot on the spot, taken away and shot, or deported.

Initially, the ghetto wasn't sealed and we could cross out of the ghetto borders to go into the other parts of the city. We were not supposed to do this but people did. By April 1940, this changed. The ghetto was officially closed. It was then wrapped in a double-barbed-wire fence. Anybody caught on the outside could be killed immediately. Anybody caught even talking to somebody on the outside or dealing with somebody on the outside could be taken to prison. We became isolated, completely cut-off, and soon, destitute and hungry.

In addition to the barbed wire fence, the Łódź ghetto was surrounded with SS guards. There were guards at sentry posts along perimeter, guards at the entry points, and guards patrolling bridges that had been constructed over two streets–Limanowskiego and Zgierska–that cut through the ghetto and allowed for general purpose "Aryan" travel. All guards carried rifles or submachine guns and had strict orders to use them. But the guards stayed mostly on the outside. They didn't come into the ghetto unless they absolutely had to or for some official action. They didn't need to come into the ghetto because the Germans had set-up a self-contained Jewish administration complete with its own large administrative staff and police force charged with enforcing all orders, rules and regulations. Adjustment to life in the ghetto was difficult. It was physically demanding and mentally trying. It was still not clear exactly what was happening to us or why and we were afraid. I, like most, knew very little about what was going on, why we were placed in the ghetto, or what the Germans were doing with us. Our lives became a course of terrible daily uncertainty that would get worse and that wouldn't end until the war's end.

Chapter 5

The Reich commissioner of the Łódź Ghetto was a man named Hans Biebow. Biebow wanted to transform the ghetto into a labor camp. He and the German authorities appointed Chaim Mordechai Rumkowski as the leader of the Jews in the Łódź ghetto. Nobody really knew why this man was chosen. Rumkowski was older, a widower who wasn't very successful in business but ran an orphanage in Helenowek. He was called the *Jüdenaelteste*, "the Eldest of the Jews," and was head of the Jewish council. He was put in charge of all ghetto social and economic life: distribution of food and medicine rations, employment, crime and punishment, deportation.

Rumkowski had his own Jewish police force, the Orderly Service. We called them "the orderlies." They wore a special armband, carried little clubs instead of guns and were charged with keeping order among those of us confined to the ghetto. Rumkowski's main role was as an intermediary between the Germans and the Jews, carrying out German directives for the creation of factories and workshops, fulfilling deportation orders, and meeting production demands.

Rumkowski created a centralized governing body and acted like an arrogant head of state. Many people despised him and blamed him for everything that would go wrong, especially the horribly disorganized food distribution and the lack of employment. But most of us were too overwhelmed with surviving to give him much thought. We were mainly concerned with finding work and getting food at any and all costs. Still, hunger and privation increased with each day and it became clear that there either wasn't enough food supplied or Rumkowski was administering it badly. People grew weary and thin and dysentery took hold. There were doctors and a hospital in the ghetto but no real medicine to speak of to help anybody.

Special money was printed in the ghetto, which was a joke. It had different denominations and Rumkowski's signature on it. We called the money "rumkies," after Rumkowski. The rumkies were worthless outside the ghetto and mostly meaningless inside the ghetto. You had to work to get money to buy ration cards to buy food. But everybody got the same ration of food anyway–about a loaf of bread per family for a week plus some rotten vegetables. And work was practically nonexistent that first year. People starved. Even with so little, over time, both the rations and available work grew even scarcer.

It was the beginning of 1940 and we were getting desperate for food. Mother didn't work. We didn't work. Not many worked at that time. Besides not getting money for rations, not working also meant you were subject to deportation. On the outskirts of the ghetto, there were some farms where Mother would go and get whatever vegetables that had been left in the ground by the farmers. She would carry them in a bag slung over her shoulder and walk the few miles back to our apartment. But this stopped. Mother returned home one day empty-handed. Our hunger grew bigger and Mother grew more frustrated.

Rumkowski used to ride proudly down the streets in a coach driven by two horses. He had his coachman at the reins and policemen flanking the sides. Occasionally, his new wife, Regina, was at his side. Regina was much younger than Rumkowski. They got married in the ghetto. One day, Mother was walking back home toward Zydowska 25, where we lived, and saw Rumkowski's coach halted on the street nearby. There were two policemen at the coach's side and one sitting with the coachman. She marched over and stood directly in front of the two horses.

"I want to talk to Rumkowski," she said to the policeman.

"You cannot talk to Rumkowski. He doesn't have the time," the policeman barked.

"But he has to make the time because I won't go away."

"Get out of the way!"

"I won't," she argued. "Give me some work. My children are starving and I am starving."

Rumkowski heard the commotion and responded, "Get her out of the way. Take her to prison if you have to." The policemen had no choice. Mother wouldn't move. They took her by both arms and dragged her away. She didn't fight them, only kept staring at Rumkowski.

The prison was located at 27 Franciszkanska Street and had been a cloister for nuns before they were forced to find other quarters. Mother stayed for a few hours and then they released her. But she didn't want to go. She told the Jewish guards, "Without a job, I have nothing to go home for but to watch my children starve. So I will stay until Rumkowski will find me a job." She stayed another hour, realized it wasn't getting her anywhere, then gave up and came home.

Employment was sporadic the entire first year. Hunger was constant. Mother, Etka, Ethel, Icek and I all registered for jobs at the Labor Department Office. While we waited, we asked around for any openings. Etka found work at a straw-shoe shop making the straw shoes that were supposed to fit over the German Army's boots when fighting in the cold. Ethel worked in a sewing shop fixing Nazi soldiers' uniforms, replacing buttons, fixing holes. Icek worked in a mechanic shop where different machines were brought for repairs. Mother initially got a job in a leather shop where saddles from horses were sent for repair or refurbishing. But I didn't find anything.

I wanted to find a way to help anyway I could. After meeting a boy named Mark who had lived down the street from us on Kilinskiego and who also had been relocated to the ghetto with his family, I thought I found a way to help. Mark was about sixteen years old, tall with dirty blonde hair and blue eyes. He looked like an Aryan and, like me, spoke fluent Polish. We first bumped into each other one day on the street. We said hello and went our separate ways. Then we ran into each other while standing in the long lines waiting to receive our ration of food. Each family was given a ration book with their family's name on it. Mark was there to get his family's rations. We chatted amiably, picked up our rations and said goodbye.

Finally, a few days later, while walking to visit Ala, my good friend from before the ghetto who now lived on the next block from us, I noticed Mark heading toward me.

He stopped and asked, "Where are you going?"

"I'm going to visit a friend," I told him.

"May I stroll along?" he asked.

I didn't mind. He started to walk with me. As we went, we talked casually, making conversation about whatever was on our minds. I felt very comfortable with him, like we had known each other for a long time. Then he abruptly paused and turned toward me. He had something important to say or ask. Confiding, he spoke of a family friend, a Polish person, an Aryan, with whom his family still had contact and who would help if he needed it. He said that he had managed to sneak out of the ghetto, get some food with some złoty his family had hidden, and smuggle the food safely back in.

I suspected why he was telling me all this, but also knew that it had become more dangerous both escaping the ghetto and walking on the streets outside. The order not to cross out of the ghetto under threat of being shot on the spot had been given, and the Germans placed more SS guards along the border and at the guard-posts to make sure they could enforce the order. Anybody who dared defy them would be made an example of. On our side, the Jewish police were also ordered to be on the lookout for people trying to get out of the ghetto. Mark was confident he could outsmart them all. He described exactly how he was able to do it without getting caught.

He told me that his plan was foolproof, that it worked every time. He said he crossed through the barbed wire fence at a place where some bushes prevented the guards from seeing him and from noticing the cut wire. From there, he said, he could quickly disappear down an adjacent side street. The key was the timing. You had to wait until the guard shift changed before you made your move. He sounded like he was an expert at this, like he had done it thousands of times. But nobody in his family wanted to go with him since the order that closed the ghetto came down.

"Even if you could get out," I told him, "How can you be sure you'll get back in?"

He must have seen the doubt and concern in my face since he spent the next few minutes assuring me that it was safe and telling me not to worry. But the expression on my face wasn't really concern for him. I knew what he was getting at. My hair was blondish, my eyes were blue, I spoke fluent Polish I was a teenager like him. He thought that the two of us could pass unseen among the Polish population, go into stores to buy things without raising any suspicion among the clerks. I knew that he wanted me to go with him. Yet, I couldn't believe it. I also couldn't believe that I wanted to do it. I was fourteen years old and impressed by what he was saying. His plan started to make sense. I imagined how nice it would be to walk into a store freely and to buy a loaf of bread and some food. One loaf of bread would go a long way. But I was hesitant and didn't speak.

"What are you thinking?" Mark asked.

I was battling and reasoning with myself. To do it would be against my nature. I wasn't brave and neither was I stupid and crossing out of the ghetto would require me to be both. I stood there convincing myself that Mark knew what he was doing, that it would be okay, that he had been successful before, that he had come home with bags full of glorious food, that I was hungry, that we were all hungry.

"What do you think?" he put the question to me directly now.

"I'll give it some thought," I told him. "I'll let you know in a day or two."

He smiled, nodded and left. I watched him disappear into the crowd, then turned and went home. I had forgotten where I was going anyway.

That night, I thought about Mark's offer. I already knew the answer but had to second-guess myself. I imagined walking into the apartment with an armload of groceries and everybody smiling at the sight. I wanted to see their smiles. I wanted to help. But, I knew I couldn't tell Mother what I was going to do. It was unthinkable, and she would absolutely forbid it. I also couldn't tell my sister, who would also forbid it. So I confided in Ethel. We were close in age, and, since she had come to live with us, had become best friends. We could tell each other anything and everything. I told her about Mark and the plan and asked her to keep it a secret. She wasn't too happy with the idea of me crossing out of the ghetto and tried to talk me out of it. But when it was clear that I couldn't be talked out of it, she promised to stand by me and help out in any way she could.

A few days passed and I saw Mark again on the street. He kept quiet and waited for me to start the conversation. By now, I was excited with my decision.

"Whenever you're ready," I told him.

He said "Good," but wanted to know if it was okay with Mother. I told him that I couldn't tell her. He was concerned about this.

"But I let my cousin in on it," I blurted.

"Okay," he nodded. He said that if I was still hesitant at any time, we could change our minds. Once on the outside, I had to be committed. I was. My mind was made up. I was eager to know when we would make the move.

"Tomorrow is as good as any day," he said.

Ethel volunteered to come along to watch out for us. She said she would hold our sweaters that had the Magen David sewn on both sides since the star had to be worn at all times inside the ghetto but once outside the ghetto it would make us a target. I didn't want her to get into any trouble, yet the thought of her being there was reassuring and holding the sweaters made sense.

We met Mark on a dirt street at the ghetto's outer edge. There were a few Jewish people passing far behind us. Ahead of us was the barbed wire fence where it intersected the bushes. Beyond the fence, there was a short open field and then a set of buildings where we planned to disappear. To the right, along the face of one of the buildings, two guards stood watch in their sentry boxes. From this distance, they appeared smaller than I knew them to be. I could see the familiar uniforms, the helmets and the machine guns. There was no turning back anymore. I silently swallowed my fear and tried to concentrate on what we were about to do.

We waited a few minutes and watched the German guards exit their posts, then head for a nearby building's doorway and disappear inside. Mark whispered, "Let's go."

We scrambled through the bushes. There were three cross beams and a wire strung in the space between each. The lower wire had been cut and buried under the dirt near the vertical fence-poles so nobody could see it hanging. It reassured me that it was as Mark said it would be. He was the first to move through the lower two posts, first one foot then the other. I followed him, moving carefully sideways on my hands and knees. I stood up and looked around before bolting across the small field and into a side street.

We made it across the field without being noticed. It was eerily silent and vacant and I could hear my heart pounding. We started down the street, hugging the side of a building as we walked around it. Then, suddenly, out of the silence came the sound of youthful voices singing in German. It was not far off, coming from an intersection just ahead. We stopped, confused about what to do next. We knew that those songs and those voices were bad news.

Mark said, "Don't worry." Very much in charge, he spoke with authority. "Remember, we're teenagers minding our own business. Smile at me and speak to me in Polish. We're just engaging in conversation."

The song grew louder and more militant as we drew closer. We saw first a line of bicycles parked on the side of the street diagonal from us. Then, we saw *them*: the SS Hitler Youth, standing proudly in their uniforms of neatly pressed breeches and sashes, diligently doing their training exercises. They were all preoccupied except one tiny and thin brown-haired boy of about ten years old who was watching us.

Mark also saw him eyeing us and whispered to me, "Keep moving. Give me your hand. Continue the conversation as before. Let's look at each other and smile, not pay any attention to them."

We had to pass a little closer and the tiny boy kept looking. Finally, he yelled out, "Jüde! Jüde!" His friends stopped and watched now too.

"Don't look at them. They want us to look at them," Mark instructed.

I did as Mark said and pretended not to notice or hear him. We smiled and walked on, innocently swinging our hands together. Once they saw that we weren't afraid of them, that we were just two teenagers who wanted to be alone and enjoy each other's company, the boy and his friends went back to their exercises. We walked out of their sight and out of any immediate danger.

Mark and I continued on. The streets started to become more familiar and I started to know where I was. A few Polish people were rushing around, going about their own business. They hardly looked at us. They hardly looked at each other. I got the sense that they too were being cautious. I suddenly wished we were home in the ghetto already, that we hadn't done this. My stomach twisted into a knot and an unsettling feeling spread through me. It was more than a feeling of anxiety, of not belonging. It was emptiness. The streets had changed. There were less people. The color was gone. Everything was gray, even the sky. I felt a sense of doom, a sense of being a stranger, a sense that everything was familiar but nothing was. I had walked freely down these streets once, unafraid. They used to be full of people whose names we knew, who we cared for, understood, loved, and with whom we shared hopes and dreams. No matter how much I tried to layer that nostalgic memory over what I was seeing and feeling, I couldn't. Łódź had been a city where life had had a purpose and was full of meaning. People worked, prospered, built their lives. Jewish and Polish alike. Now the place was completely empty of Jews; not many Polish people either besides the cautious few. I felt like a ghost among ghosts. The city where we were born, lived, grew up, thrived was a stranger. Unrecognizable, gone.

It had only been a few months since the Germans entered the city, since I had last seen Father, since the terror began and since we had been herded into the ghetto. But it felt like years because in those short few months, everything changed. And even though time surely passed once second after another, I had aged years in just those few months. Like other children, I had to say the most improper, hasty goodbye to every facet of my childhood existence and now found myself a fugitive in my own city.

Mark and I walked further until we spied a bakery up ahead. He told me to wait outside while he went to buy bread and a few rolls. He unrolled two canvas bags he had shoved into his pockets and handed them to me to hold. He went into the bakery. I stood alone on the street, nervous, afraid and trying not to show it. Some minutes passed and Mark emerged from the bakery with some bread and rolls. I put them into the bags and we moved on.

"Was it okay?" I asked.

"The sales lady was very friendly. She even smiled at me as she handed me the items," he said.

Further down the street, there was another food store. Mark handed me some money. "It's your turn," he said.

A little reluctant, I nevertheless found the courage and walked in. A portly woman with thick round curls stood near the door. She made me nervous. I said, *dzien dobry*, Polish for good morning. She responded *dzien dobry*, and then asked me what I wanted to buy.

The brief exchange – so normal, so mundane – filled me with the smallest happiness. I wasn't really ready for her to be cordial and hadn't thought ahead of time about what I wanted. So I quickly pointed at a few items here and there, doing my best to stay in character. I paid the lady, said *dowidzenia*, see you again, and exited. Outside, Mark smiled. Nothing to worry about.

We stopped in a third and final store and went in together. We bought another loaf of bread and other items. Our bags were full. We had accomplished what we had come for. We turned back toward the ghetto, being careful to travel mostly deserted streets.

Near the ghetto border we stopped and looked ahead. We could see between the buildings that a guard was standing at the sentry post. He was watching dutifully over his area, the area with the open lot we needed to cross to get back to the place where Mark had cut the fence wire. I was more scared than ever and clutched the bag of food firmly in my arms. My throat dried and seized into a tight bundle. Mark talked calmly to me to ease my tension.

"Don't worry. You know what to do," he told me.

He may have felt as afraid as me but he didn't show it. He acted poised and in command. We waited and watched for what seemed like forever. Overhead, the sky had grown thick with dark clouds that threatened any second to open up and pour down a heavy rain. I wanted to get home before it started. I felt like a thief, hiding and waiting for the right moment to make a move. I could hear the Hitler Youth in the distance, still enthusiastically chanting, singing, shouting. Just then, the guard turned away to put on his raincoat and we made our move.

We walked quickly along a building then into the open lot. The sky thundered and broke open with a pounding rain. The drops hit thick on the dirt beneath our shoes, turning it quickly into sticky mud. We picked up our pace to a slight jog when, through the sound of the rain falling, came a tinny voice, "Jüde! Jüde stop!" It rang out accompanied by what sounded like a thousand metallic whistles blowing. It was the Hitler Youth. They were coming quickly our way, chasing and blowing their SS-issued whistles. In the front of the group was the tiny brown-haired boy. We started running full speed. A group of the sentry guards emerged from a doorway holding their madly barking dogs.

I glanced back and saw Mark running a little behind me and the dogs and soldiers starting to give chase behind him. We doubled our speed as we ran for our lives. The rain pounded. The ground became wetter, the mud thicker. We reached the short field before the ghetto fence. I could see the bushes and the opening in the fence ahead. I pumped my legs with everything I had, with all my might and breath. Then I heard a thud and turned quickly to see Mark lying face down in the mud, clutching tightly to the bags of food. He had slipped and fallen. The guards with their dogs were getting closer. A rifle shot rang out. Mark tried to get up but slipped and fell again. He shoved his bag of bread at me.

"Go!" he said. "I'll be right behind you. I'll catch up to you." I hesitated. He insisted, "Go!"

I grabbed the bags and sprinted. "Jüde, stop!" I heard again this time from a guard. "Stop or I will shoot you!"

I wasn't stopping. Then I heard the echoing pops of gunfire behind me. I glanced back but couldn't see Mark. He wasn't behind me. The guards had slowed their chase but were still coming. I ran, not looking back again, my feet splashing in tiny puddles, each stride and footfall sticking in the mud below. It grabbed onto one of my shoes and ripped it off my foot, but I kept going. The barking dogs were getting louder and closer. I finally reached the barbed wire fence, out of breath and hyperventilating. I dropped to my knees and crawled between the fence rails. Then I blacked out.

I don't know how long I was unconscious before I opened my eyes to see my cousin Ethel kneeling over me, her wet hair framed by the gray sky. Beside her, were two Jewish orderlies. One had his arms crossed; the other stood cradling something beneath his coat. They both looked extremely displeased.

The rain was still falling heavily and I was soaked. I sat up and realized that the German guards hadn't given up on me. I could hear their cursing and their dogs as they paced the fence border trying to figure out where I went. Apparently, as I later learned from Ethel, I had made it through the fence, emerged from the bushes and collapsed.

I thought of Mark and looked at Ethel. Starting to ask her, I saw the small crowd of people that had gathered around us and stopped. The German guards approached the section where Mark had cut the wire. Ethel handed me my sweater and whispered to put it on quickly.

Still disoriented, I obeyed, remembering the yellow star. One of the guards called over one of the orderlies.

He began speaking to the orderly who responded by making gestures like he didn't know what the guard was talking about. Then the other orderly who was still standing near me looked down and said, "See what this causes." I looked up and could now see that he had the bag of food pinned between his arm and his side, concealed under his raincoat. I looked down and noticed my shoe was missing.

At the fence, the other orderly was still making exasperated gestures like he didn't know anything. Finally he walked back over to us. He immediately came down on me, scolding. "Do you want to get everybody punished?"

Then the other joined in, lecturing. "You know you are not supposed to leave the ghetto."

"They want us to hand over the culprit," the first one said.

I looked up at him and over to Ethel. I didn't know what to say and so just waited and listened.

"I told them we didn't know who it was but that we would find the girl and hand her over," the orderly said. He motioned toward my shoeless foot. "They'll have your footprint in the mud. Your shoe. It will be easy to prove."

Ethel, normally mousey and quiet, blurted "Take me in her place. My foot is much smaller. They'll see that they made a mistake."

"Little girl, stay with your cousin," the orderly barked.

He walked briskly back over to the guards and said something. The guards turned and started back for their posts. I don't know what the orderly said. I don't know why the guards walked away. Like the orderly warned, had they pursued me into the ghetto they would have seen my lack of shoe and known I was guilty. Maybe they wanted to get in out of the rain. Maybe they thought the Jewish orderlies would handle it. I was in shock, still not believing that Mark was not here. I asked Ethel where he was. She was in tears. "I didn't see him," was all she could say.

The policeman told Ethel to run home and retrieve Mother. Exhausted, I staggered to my feet. My clothes were heavy and soggy. I stood there wet and with only one shoe on my feet. Ethel came quickly back with Mother a few steps ahead. She had already explained what happened. Mother had a pair of shoes with her and made me change into them immediately. Then she thanked the two policemen. They gave us a loaf of bread and a roll and confiscated the rest of the bag of food. They told me that I was foolish but lucky and warned me never to do it again.

Back in our ghetto apartment, Mother wanted to know the whole story. As I described what happened, Icek and Etka also sat listening. Etka told me I should be thankful I'm alive. I agreed. I was thankful and happy to be alive but when Mother asked me about Mark, I couldn't bring myself to talk. She saw this and didn't force me to say any more. Instead, she kissed me and said, "Thank God you are alive and home with your family." Then she told me to get some rest. I lay down on the bed, tossing back and forth, crying myself to sleep.

Chapter 6

The Germans officially annexed the city of Łódź into the Reich and renamed it Litzmannstadt. Technically, according to the Germans, we were in the "Litzmannstadt" ghetto not the Łódź ghetto. But to us it was the Łódź ghetto. At first, the ghetto inhabitants came only from Łódź and the immediately surrounding areas. Then, as years passed, Jews from other parts of Europe arrived. They came from recently dissolved ghettos or just new conquered places in the Reich. They newer arrivals never adjusted well to ghetto life. They arrived with their healthy cheeks, nice coats and suitcases, saw what we were going through, were instantly horrified, and volunteered to be on the next transport out figuring that even a labor camp would be better than this place. Of course, they weren't always taken to labor camps, as we later learned. More and more Jews arrived from all over until, at the final count, over one hundred sixty thousand were squeezed into those few square miles.

We had no good news to latch onto in the ghetto because there wasn't any news to have, good or bad. We had no connection to what was going on in other ghettos or other parts of the world. Trapped and hermetically cut-off, we didn't know what was happening with the war, what was going on in the camps, anything. Zero information came into the Łódź ghetto until the Germans and Viennese and Czechs and Hungarians and provincial Poles started to arrive and bring tidbits of news with them. For the most part, and as far as I was personally aware, it was a complete existence of forced ignorance. I never knew of anybody to have a radio or a newspaper from the outside (both illegal), though some people probably did.

We were dying by the thousands. Most of the dwellings were extremely run-down and old. The clayish walls of the buildings were rotten. Many times the lower floors or basement floors would flood and the walls would just crumble from the bottom up. The apartments were cramped one-room or two-room places. There were few sanitary facilities like bathrooms or showers in the apartments. Usually, there were three or four toilets off of the courtyard or on the lower floor of a building or people just used nearby outhouses. There was no sewage system. Sanitation was also sorely lacking even though you couldn't tell by looking at the streets. Keeping clean streets was Rumkowski's way of showing the Germans he was being vigilant about taking care to prevent disease even though everywhere you looked you saw the sick and the dying.

The living conditions in the ghetto were merciless and severely inhuman. The most basic of necessities were nowhere to be found. It was irrational and impractical to treat a workforce this way, to let them starve and die of disease. But, their thinking exceeded even the logic of practicality; it was the logic of the worst arrogance, hatred, cruelty and madness, of an evil too great to be previously imagined. It was a premeditated program of slow death through deprivation, starvation, and sickness. The ghetto achieved the same goal as the crematoria would and did, but more slowly and without the heavy lifting. Resistance, in the face of these conditions, was impossible. We had nothing to fight with. How could we get guns? Who had the strength? We believed we were safe as long as we worked.

After a few months of working at the leather and straw shoe workshops, a new opportunity was presented for Mother and Etka through *protectia*. *Protectia* was a network of connections of influential people. Aunt Fradla, who was in the ghetto with us, had many connections. One was with an influential man named David Gertler. Gertler was head of the Jewish Special Unit (*Sonderkommando*), a powerful ghetto organization loosely associated with the Orderly Service, but it was in fact independent. Gertler was somewhat of a rival to Rumkowski's authority, and, in some ways, was the more effective administrator. The Germans put him in charge of certain parts of the economy in 1942 and things went much more smoothly. The vegetable distribution, for instance, was more on time, better organized and less spoiled. Eventually in 1943, Gertler disappeared. Nobody knew whether he was deported, killed, or had escaped.

It happened that when we had to register in the ghetto, the person who registered us made a mistake and put an accidental "r" in our name. "Getler" became "Gertler." We saw small advantages like receiving better quality rations because of the new association with David Gertler. Indirectly it helped us, so we decided not to correct it.

Aunt Fradla and Uncle Heskel had been well acquainted with David Gertler before the war. In the ghetto, when we needed jobs, She wrote a note recommending us to him. She gave the note to Etka, who delivered it to his office. Gertler's cousin, who was in charge of a place called Molkerai, was able to get Etka and Mother jobs there. Molkerai was where vegetables were processed for distribution in the ghetto. It was located in Marysin. Marysin was a plot of land adjacent to the ghetto that was comprised mostly of open fields, a few small factories and barracks or clapboard houses. The area was annexed to the ghetto as part of Rumkowski's "refuge through work" program. Second-hand frozen and spoiled potatoes and other vegetables were sent to Molkerai for processing. Mother and Etka worked in the division that made salads out of the rotten food. The salads were later distributed to the places where we received our weekly rations. When Marysin was finally closed, the salads stopped being part of our rations.

Mother and Etka received a daily food card while at their job. With it, they got a bowl of watery soup. This helped make it so Ethel, Icek and my portion of our weekly bread ration could be a little bigger at home. It was a small thing but small things counted in that time of starvation. Occasionally too, when nobody was looking, Mother and Etka helped themselves to some cooked potatoes and vegetables.

At the time, I was not working and Mother and Etka were very scared for me. People who didn't work were in more danger of being deported because they were considered unproductive. Eventually I found out through Labor Services that there was an opening at a small rug-weaving workshop that had been set up in Marysin. I thought I would give it a try. At first I was hesitant. I had never worked before and I didn't know if I could do what was required. I was scared that I wouldn't be hired but I went anyway being more scared of the possibility of being deported.

I walked all the way to Marysin, about twenty or thirty minutes from Zydowska Street, mulling over these doubts in my head. Before I knew it, I was standing outside the door to a place we called Klugman's. I went right inside to an office of sorts. It was a small, ramshackle anteroom with a ratty old wooden desk and chair. Through a doorway, I could see a hint of the space where the workers were sitting on stools weaving rugs that were hanging on walls. I paced back and forth, waiting, when Roza, a supervisor, entered from the workshop. She was about twenty years old, tall and beautiful with big blue eyes and long blond, wavy hair that flowed down past her shoulders. She had a gentle yet confident look about her and smiled as she spoke.

"Are you waiting for somebody or would you like something?"

I said, "Yes. I came here… I heard they are hiring and I would like to get a job."

She asked me my name. I told her "Masha." Then she asked me my age. I told her "Fifteen." She didn't ask me what I did or didn't know about making rugs because most of the people who came to work had to learn on the job.

She said, "How would you like to start tomorrow?"

"Okay," I said.

I could not believe it. I ran home happy and proud. I wanted to share the good news. Mother was very happy for me. We didn't get paid but we were able to get our small food rations, plus working meant I was not supposed to be subject to deportation, that I could stay in the ghetto with my family.

The next morning, I woke up at about 5:00 a.m. and went to my first day on the job. I didn't know what to expect but I was eager and curious. When I arrived, I saw many people already there, busily weaving the rugs. The workshop was a largish, open space. There were piles of colored rags on the floor or in bags or strewn about on some high tables in the middle of the room. On the walls hung frames of wires onto which the rags were being woven in patterns for the rugs. The rugs came in sizes: small, medium and large. At each of the frames, there were instructors, *instruktorkas*, who were all women, standing with a group of other workers. The *instruktorkas* were reviewing patterns or showing people how to weave the edges so they wouldn't fray.

Roza was the supervisor on the floor and introduced me to the process of making the rugs. She laid it out gently but firmly: "Our job is to make rugs with these rags, woven by hand, to fill the orders sent in by the Germans. The orders must be filled by the *exact date* specified. It is my responsibility to see to this, so it's not something you should worry about. Myself or another floor supervisor will inspect all the rugs. If they are not made correctly, they will be shipped back to us and this is bad."

I liked Roza immediately. She was kind and patient but tough. I didn't consider it unusual that the rugs were made from rags. Nothing went to waste in the ghetto. Roza set me up by showing me how to do the weaves and follow the patterns. My first week was all practice. My biggest fear was that the work I was doing wouldn't pass inspection so I was careful to do everything right. At first I worked on smaller, triangle-shaped rugs. Roza was impressed with my work and allowed me to then quickly progress to larger rugs, choosing my own colors for simple patterns.

Roza was an artist and very much a perfectionist. She took pride in doing a good job. For many of us in the ghetto, the work we did kept our minds off of being hungry and afforded some solace from the day-to-day fears and anxieties. At the rug shop Roza's talent had a chance to be expressed. She sketched and created her own designs and patterns. They were usually more complicated and impressive than other people's designs.

Near the end of the week, Roza came over and watched me work. It made me nervous but I was happy to have the chance to try to impress her. She watched me selecting colors for rugs. I would choose the colors very carefully–brown with yellow or green with blue. I didn't know anything about what colors worked technically better with other colors. I just thought about it for a minute and chose what I figured would look nice together. Roza was impressed that I was taking the time to think about what I was doing. She sat down next to me on a bench and said, "I'm working now on a very special project. It's an order for a very large rug for a high-ranking German SS officer and the deadline for when the rug is to be complete is very near. To make sure it is met, I will be working on it myself. It is a special and difficult design and I would like you to work on it with me."

She said that I could work on the corners while she worked on the main part. I could also help her to fill in the backgrounds. I was astonished and honored that she wanted me to help her with such an important project. Her confidence and trust in me filled me with confidence and trust in myself. She said my first job every morning would be to pull the proper colors of rags from the bags and have them ready when she arrived. Then I would help her by starting to work on the corners of the pattern, a pattern she designed herself. It was beautiful and intricate. Every night she took the design home with her so that it wouldn't get lost or ruined by the second shift. The shop was running basically two shifts each day and night to keep up with production demands.

The next day, we started work on the carpet. Each day, Roza would come in and place her design for the pattern of the rug next to the frame. Gradually, the pattern started to take shape. It was a challenge to work with Roza. She was fast and good at what she did and I did my best to keep up with my job of filling in the corners and background. She always seemed to be ahead of me. She'd often look up from her work at me as if to say playfully, "C'mon, keep up."

After about two weeks of working on the rug, I came in one morning and Roza wasn't there. Another *instruktorka* told me that Roza had come down with the flu. She said Roza hoped to be back in a few days and that if I had any work left to do I should do it. If not, she was going to give me another rug to work on. I didn't want to work on another rug, so I told her I had enough still to do to keep me busy until Roza returned. I had always worked under Roza's supervision and review. Now I had to guide myself and catch my own mistakes. Continuing with the background, I worked slowly and methodically, being careful not to mess up.

A few days passed. I was nearing the end of my work on the background but Roza was still absent. I worried that the main part of the design still had to be woven and wondered if another *Instruktorka* would fill in for Roza so that the rug would be finished on time. I didn't know exactly when the deadline was but I didn't want Roza to get in trouble so I asked one of the other *instruktorkas* if she could help me. But she had no idea how to complete the pattern. The design was in Roza's possession. Besides, she told me, it was Roza's project. It would have to wait until Roza got back.

Something came over me then, the sense of a challenge I had to meet. I thought, "Let me see how far I can go with this." I figured that I could always take apart whatever wasn't right. Determined and desperate to meet the unknown but impending deadline, I continued to work on the entire pattern completely from memory. Amazingly, the design started to come alive before my eyes. I doubled my focus on all the details, becoming nearly obsessed and working nonstop. I filled in the entire middle face of the pattern and then moved on to the background and corners. Some of the floor supervisors passed by and gazed in disbelief at the design taking shape. The background and corners would take me about another two days but now I knew I could complete the job.

I worked feverishly the entire next day in an attempt to complete the design. It was almost finished—there was just one corner to complete—when Roza showed up. I was so excited and happy to see her and so nervous and uneasy at the same time. I had no idea how she would react to what I had done or if the work would pass her inspection and approval. Before I had a chance to speak, Roza was standing there holding up her design and comparing it to the rug. She couldn't believe the accuracy.

"How did you do it?" she asked.

I said, "I really don't know. I must have remembered or something."

She was so thrilled she kissed me. She was proud that I was capable of remembering and carrying out the design that she had created. "It's perfect," she said. "I'm so happy and proud of you."

In another day the rug was finished, inspected and readied for delivery. The time Roza and I spent working together was a nice break from all that was going on in the ghetto. To be sure, there was no escaping the hunger or the suffering on people's faces, but the work kept us busy. Through Roza's recommendation and the recommendation of the other *instruktorkas*, at fifteen years old, I became the youngest *instruktorka* at Klugman's.

I worked long, arduous hours at the rug shop, but at least time passed less noticeably. Once, we even received an order from Rumkowski himself. The king wanted a rug. It was to be large and have a special design on it. Two other *instruktorkas* and I, together with a few of our better workers, were selected to make the rug. Rumkowski's rug ended up being the biggest I'd ever worked on. Normally we could hang anywhere from three to six frames of varying sizes on the workshop wall, but this rug's frame covered almost all of it. We worked in teams on different sections and in two shifts. The work was constantly going on this rug. It seemed odd to me that among all this decimation of the Jewish people, Rumkowski wanted a rug. But we completed the job and sent it off to him.

Family and Friends in the countryside. Helenowek, Poland. Circa 1933.

*(Left to Right) Shlomo, Paula (friend of Etka), Marian, Mother, Etka.
At the Canteen in the DP Camp, Neustadt Holstein.*

Mother, Shlomo, Marian. Canteen in the DP Camp, Neustadt Holstein.

Marian passport photo taken in Nestadt Holstein, Germany. Circa 1947.

Marian. Photo taken at Jewish Cemetery in Cleveland. 1966.

Aunt Mania. Taken most probably in 1935 in Lodz Poland.
Photo received from Moshe Bogen after the war.

Mother, after liberation, Neustadt Holstein, 1945 or 1946.

Mother. 1946 Winter. Neustadt Holstein.

Funeral procession in the DP camp.
Neustadt Holstein. Late 1945 or 1946.

Funeral procession in the DP camp.
Neustadt Holstein. Late 1945 or 1946.

Cemetery in Neustadt Holstein.

Cemetery in Neustadt Holstein. Marian at stone setting.
Photo taken by British Soldier after the liberation. Late 1945 or 1946.

Marian and Isak wedding in Rochester, NY. April 29, 1956.

Chuck's Bar Mitzvah. 1960.
(Left to Right) Isak, Marian, Chuck and Mother.

Marian and Isak. Taken at youngest son, Jack's Bar Mitzvah. 1974.

Mother and Abe.

Marian's son Chuck. College graduation

Marian's daughter Nancy.
High school graduation.

Marian's daughter Anita.
High school graduation.

Marian's son Jack.
High school graduation.

Nancy. Graduation from Shaarei Tzedek Hospital. Jerusalem.

Chuck and Marian at Chuck's daughter Lisa's wedding. 2003

Marian and Etka at wedding. June 29, 2003.

Chapter 7

Every day in the ghetto we faced a new law or ordinance, some new hardship to add to the already overwhelming hardships. We never knew what to expect, what tomorrow would bring. I tried my best to remain hopeful through it all, to remain human and faithful to God. I was very lucky that my family was relatively together and that I had good people around who had a good impact on me. Once, in the ghetto, an old man was standing downstairs and asked me if I could spare a piece of bread. His face was unwashed and gaunt with a scrappy beard. His clothes seemed rattier than most. I thought that maybe something was wrong with him. I went upstairs and took a piece of bread, the piece I was supposed to keep for myself for a whole week, and gave it to him. I didn't tell anybody about it.

The next morning came. Everybody was eating but me. Mother asked me "Masha, why aren't you eating? Where is your bread?"

I told her somebody came and I gave it to him. She said, "Masha, but everybody has the same portion, everybody in the ghetto has the same portion. What are you going to eat now?"

Exasperated, they all shared their portions with me. I wasn't thinking when I gave the man my bread. It was an automatic response. Mother used to say, "If somebody's hungry, you give them bread. No matter who comes into a house, be it rich or poor, if he comes in and stretches out his hand, give him something. Don't ask questions." This was part of who I was. I could not take the suffering of others.

I took a walk, as I sometimes did, down Zydowska Street, then turned to cut through an alley just before Stary Rynek, a public square where Etka, early on in our time in the ghetto, witnessed the horrifying sight of two men being hanged. I was heading toward Wolborska Street where the oldest and most beautiful synagogue in the city had once stood. The building was elegant, finely detailed in its stonework, stunning. Inside it was cavernous and able to house the hundreds of worshipers who would came to pray and study. It was a landmark of religious life. Now it was an empty lot, a pile of bombed rubble, broken stones, gravel and fallen walls–a victim of the systematic German dynamiting.

Seeing the ruins there, under the gray-blue sky, pain pierced my heart. Shivers ran up my spine. I recalled the faces of the many people on the streets, coming and going, the way they looked just happy, tranquil, hopeful, conversing with their families and friends, glad to be with them. I then thought of the beggars who would wait outside the entrance on weekdays to ask for handouts from the pious men praying inside. I remember being a little girl running to give pennies to these beggars, crying when I didn't have enough pennies for everybody. It was uncomfortable to see people so ragged, crippled or blind. I wanted to help all of them. I tried not to stare for fear that I would shame them. Now, as I stood across from the wrecked building, I felt that we had all become beggars. We were all one class of people. There were no shamefaced little girls crying to hand us pennies. I was not that little girl anymore.

There was rarely joy among us in the ghetto. Depression and anxiety were rampant. Nights were especially difficult. Where we lived, I heard such violent screams, as if somebody was cutting somebody else to pieces. I don't know who or what the screams were coming from, maybe girls being raped, or men being tortured by the *Kripo*, or people being murdered, or just the sounds of hunger or some other kind of slow, painful dying. You could hear the cries and screams every night. They would come from somewhere further away, muted but still piercing. I never knew, I never saw the place where any of it was happening, where the sounds originated from, but they were present from the beginning and persisted through to the end. I still remember hearing them as I tried to sleep and the feeling of hollowness, of emptiness, powerlessness, of disbelieving what I was hearing. It was in my consciousness then, my awareness. Now, in my subconscious, these screams live with me. They sounded like they were coming from another world but they were coming from this world. I have never heard anything like them since.

In the winter of 1941 life grew especially hard. It was bitterly cold. Nobody was ever on the streets. And fewer people showed up to work at Klugman's. Heating in the ghetto buildings was always problematic. We received coal rations, but they were too meager for even one night. People were dying from the cold, literally freezing to death. Desperation grew to a pitch. People tore down whatever they could find that would burn: fences, parts of buildings, empty houses, even ripping apart pieces of their own buildings. Gradually the landscape became more sparse and broken down as these things were burned as fuel for heat.

One day, on her way back from getting our coal rations, Etka was halted in her tracks by an abhorrent scene. She saw people being loaded onto wagons, mostly women and children. She couldn't believe the way they were being treated. The Germans manhandled them, tossed them around, shoved them into their trucks and wagons. Some were shot right there on the street where they stood. Etka hurried away and when she came home was in tears. This was our first real experience of the deportation actions–through Etka's tears.

We consoled ourselves with the thought that the deportees were just being sent to work at different places. This is what we were told, made to believe, frightened into accepting. Even though our instincts said that this was a lie, we had no way of knowing for sure. In our minds it was crazy to lose workers, slave labor for the German war effort. Plus, throughout the life of the ghetto, Rumkowski assured us that by turning the Łódź Jews into a workforce for the German Reich, we would be saved and protected. There were always struggles and random deportations but Rumkowski, with Biebow's help, seemed to achieve some semblance of his "refuge through work" program. The ghetto factories and workshops were numerous and supported every kind of industry. Far from being just another ghetto, Łódź became the largest labor camp in Europe. Nevertheless, the deportation actions started. The Germans announced that in order to ensure our continued refuge and to promote productivity, children, the sick and elderly, as unproductive members of the workforce, had to be removed. We were told that they would be resettled in a safer place with better conditions.

Rumkowski told people not to worry and to voluntarily hand over the children. But parents became frightened and confused by this new order. They didn't understand why or how somebody could ask a mother or father to "voluntarily" give up their children even if it was only temporary and to a "better" place. Most parents hid their children when the orderlies came around to gather them. They argued, begged and pleaded, "How can you send out my child when your own child does not have to be sent out?" The orderlies assured the parents that the children would be cared for and safe. But parents didn't care. Ultimately, the orderlies were unwilling to take the children by force, and when it became clear that deportation quotas weren't being met, the Germans took over the removal process. They did it with surprise blockades and raids. Parents on the streets ran from them in a panic grasping children in their arms, trying to escape and hide. The Germans went house-to-house, door-to-door taking children by force, many times at night, ripping the child from a bed or a distraught Mother's arms. Even the orphanages were emptied out.

After they swept the ghetto for children, they turned their focus to the sick and elderly, which concerned us because Mother had just gotten over pneumonia and still appeared pale, thin and fragile. Then it happened. One of the German raids for the sick and elderly occurred on our street, at our address, Zydowska 25. The SS did their usual unexpected rushing entry, driving wagons and trucks into the street, closing the street at both ends, and firing a pistol into the air while barking orders to get out. "Jüde get out! Jüde!" It was like a nightmare that word, hearing it all the time shouted from the mouths of German soldiers and SS or in the metallic echo of a loudspeaker mounted on a truck. "*Jüde*! Get out or you will be shot!"

Jews flowed out of their buildings, scared, hunched over, skinny, hungry, in tattered clothes, with forlorn faces. We did the same until there was one long line of people standing at attention all the way down the street. Etka, Ethel, Icek and I were terribly frightened, plus we had come out of the building without Mother.

When we had heard the initial pistol shot and call on the loudspeaker, "Jüde come out!" we scrambled around in a frantic search for some rouge to put on Mother's pale cheeks. We were scared that she wouldn't pass the inspection in her post-pneumonia state. The thought of watching her loaded onto the wagons and taken away made me sick. But there was no rouge anywhere and we were running out of time. I heard banging on the doors of one of the nearby buildings. Next would be the boots stomping up our own building's staircase, a door slamming open and the sound of a revolver going off pointed at each one of us. Mother quickly shoved us out the door. She insisted she had a plan and said that she would be okay. We had no choice but to hurry outside and line up.

Standing there on the street, I watched as the Germans emptied the rest of the buildings, going inside each one to search for hiders. Completing the search, they would exit, sometimes dragging people out, and close and lock the building's doors behind them to signal that the building had been cleared. Behind me, I glanced at a group of soldiers entering our apartment house. I closed my eyes and waited for the crack of the revolver that would tell me Mother was killed. But nothing happened. It was quiet for what seemed like an eternity. Then the soldiers came out and locked our building. No Mother.

It was chilly that day and the sun burned the sky white, casting harsh, angular shadows across the ground. I peered through the glare and watched as the SS men went down the line of people doing inspections, pulling the unlucky and unfortunate out of line and shoving them onto wagons. I braced as they moved closer to us. Would I be sent out or not? Would Etka? Ethel? Icek?

They came upon Ethel first. She was standing a little to the side and in front of me. An SS man pointed at her. She was ordered onto the wagon. My heart trembled and I bit my lip to keep from yelling out as she walked slowly over to the wagon. They had Ethel and I could do nothing except watch. Next, they came to me. As they were looking me over, another SS man abruptly pulled Ethel off of the wagon. I don't know what happened or if they just had a change of heart, but Ethel was told to stand back in line. She passed. They moved on without putting me on the wagon. I passed also. Etka passed as well. They stopped at Icek and talked to each other about something. Icek was about fourteen, still young but tall. I wanted to shout out that he was working, that he had a job and they shouldn't take him. I didn't say anything. Icek passed and they moved on.

The four of us stood there and watched as the SS continued down the line. I saw our next-door neighbors, a young couple with their little daughter of about six years old. She must have been kept well out of sight. I had never seen the girl before and I don't know why she still wasn't hidden. The little girl was very pretty. She had wide, blue eyes and long blonde hair that curled at the end, just lightly tipping the top of her shoulders. The girl was dressed in her best dress, had on shiny black shoes, and wore a pretty blue ribbon in her hair. Seeing the SS interest in her daughter, the girl's mother's eyes widened with desperation, a silent plea that would fall on deaf ears. The SS grabbed the girl and loaded her onto the wagon.

The little girl looked at them, puzzled, then back at her father and mother who now choked back profound, silent tears. The mother's eyes turned instantly from hopeful to morose, cold, distant, detached. And her father's face became withdrawn, emptiness so present in his eyes that they appeared defeated, forlorn, ghostly. From one minute to the next, you could see the isolation and despondence take hold, the spirit drain out of their bodies. The dress, the ribbon, the curls framing the girl's innocent face were the hope that somewhere down the line, this pretty, handsomely dressed, beribboned little girl would be taken in or spared a terrible fate by a merciful soul. It was a last ditch effort to wrap her up in a glorious shroud and send her down the river, like the baby Moses, into the arms of a compassionate stranger.

We watched as others of our neighbors were looked over, the SS moving ever methodically down the line of faces, plucking them like leaves from a tree branch. This person to the wagon, this person to stand with the group who passed. The next one to stand with the group who passed, that one to the wagon. This person cries silently, that person withdraws silently. This person hopes a better fate awaits. That person knows there is no better fate.

I looked away from the faces of those being sent out. I wanted each one to pass inspection and come stand with us but it couldn't be so. It was a tragedy unfolding before me. I had heard, seen, and now lived it. I felt sad but lucky that I wasn't leaving in one of those trucks with those mercenaries of death. And I was terribly preoccupied thinking about Mother.

After the selection was over, they opened the doors to our buildings and let us return. We sped inside, wanting to see Mother and find out what happened. To our relief and surprise, she was in our apartment waiting for us. She was thrilled and relieved to see us all there, alive and safe. "Thank God," she said. We were also thrilled and relieved and eager to know what happened.

She told us that, at the last minute, she decided to go down to the lavatory on the first floor. There were three toilets with partitions there and she sat on the furthest one from the door, hoping that between the darkness of the room and the unwillingness of the guards to enter all the way, she would go unnoticed. If they found her, she would have told them that she had terrible cramps and couldn't come out. She wasn't alone either. There were a few neighbors in the lavatory with her but when they heard a guard shout in the doorway, "Whoever is hiding, come out or you will be shot!" they got scared and went out right away.

Despite the warning, Mother remained still, not moving from her place. When the guards saw the others exit the lavatory, they didn't search any further. Mother knew she had to wait until the selection was over, so she listened for the sound of doors opening. When she heard them and then saw people returning, she went up to the apartment to wait for us. We couldn't believe her courage and were happy to still be together. But it was in this deportation action that Uncle Hershel, Mother's youngest brother, lost his wife Hela and their children. Hela like many mothers wouldn't let her children be taken so she was taken with them. They would later be murder at Chelmno.

The Germans continued the deportation actions until they were satisfied that only an able-bodied workforce remained. Thousands were removed from the ghetto, but not all of the children were caught. Many remained, successfully hidden in cellars and attics or other inventive places. With the scale of these deportations, it became harder to convince myself that the Germans were taking people any place other than to their deaths. Afterward, the change in the countenance of people on the streets was undeniable. Mothers and fathers having lost their children walked around like shells of human beings. Others who had lost loved ones just appeared endlessly disconsolate.

After this deportation action, the deportations stopped for a while. But everything changed irreversibly after it. What was bad grew worse as conditions deteriorated and people died all around us. We entered a period of work, starvation, and disease. There was nothing else. During this time, Uncle Hershel became extremely ill. His emaciated, weakened body swelled up. I remember his feet and face ballooning and becoming contorted, red, and flush, as he lay there, motionless on his bed. Mother, Etka, Ethel and I all took turns caring for him, sitting at his bedside in shifts. Occasionally, he would burst out moaning and writhing and then suddenly stop, staring quietly wide-eyed at the ceiling, vacantly grasping for each breath.

It was the dead of winter and freezing all around. Keeping him warm was next to impossible. One day when it was my turn to be with him, his body began to shake violently. He started crying out incoherently. I jumped up in shock, not knowing what to do. Moments later, he was silent, dead. He had been terribly ill, but I didn't expect him to die. I had never witnessed this before, never known the actual moment of death so up close and personal. Did the outcry mean he was suffering, or was it normal? Not knowing what to do, I left in a hurry and went to find Mother.

Chapter 8

After a while, the Marysin workshops were closed or moved and general activity was consolidated to the more central parts of the ghetto. Klugman's was moved to Wolborska Street. While the new location was much easier for me to walk to from our apartment, the space was also much smaller. As an *instruktorka*, I was placed in charge of a group of teenagers aged twelve to sixteen who had so far escaped the deportations. Being in charge of them was strange since I was their age. Yet it also worked well because we could relate to each other. I didn't pressure them and tried to help as much as I could. I taught them how to make the rugs properly and how to repair their mistakes. But the mistakes were numerous and the rugs were frequently badly finished or incomplete. Often I'd have to finish the work for them.

Working with the other teenagers was simultaneously painful and joyous. Seeing the faces of those whose loved ones had been sent out of the ghetto or who had died was difficult. Seeing the worry and seriousness and gravity in their eyes was also painful. But for those hours that we were together, just the group of us, unsupervised except by me, we felt like children again. We'd laugh and sing songs while we worked. We identified and related to each other. We could act and feel our own ages, like teen-agers, like children.

I had a few friends in the ghetto and counted some of the Klugman's group among them. There was a girl named Franka, an unusually beautiful girl who was sent out in one of the first transports. There was also Edzia Klugman, Klugman's niece, who was a little older than me. She was also an *instruktorka* at the workshop. Pola Zilberberg was in my group at Klugman's as well. Most of her family had already been deported. Her brother was still with her but he was very sick with tuberculosis. She was always worried because she didn't have anything for him, nothing to nourish him or help make him well. Etka didn't eat her portion of bread one day, so I tried to give it to Pola, thinking maybe she could give it to her brother. For some reason she wouldn't take it. I don't know what happened to her, but her brother died in the ghetto. Sometimes Edzia, Pola, and myself would get together outside of Klugman's with another two girls, Fela Adlic and Rysia. Rysia was an artist with the most beautiful, delicate features. We were all about the same age and enjoyed each other's company immensely, but little by little, one by one, we lost this friend or that friend and there was no way to keep in touch.

There was one girl in my work group at Klugman's named Malka. She was about twelve or thirteen years old. She was waif-like and completely withdrawn. She never spoke, not even when spoken to. It was always like her mind was somewhere else or deep in thought, like something so tragic had happened that she couldn't muster enough voice to speak. Malka didn't do great work and had no desire to learn. She would sit against the wall, sorting idly through rags. She didn't care to make an effort because she had passed the point where she cared about anything. We all helped by finishing her work for her, even though everybody was busy with her own work and concerns. Most of the time we couldn't even be sure what we would find when we got home at the end of a shift. If we were lucky, everybody who was there in the morning was still there in the evening. I wanted to help Malka and gave her the permanent assignment of simply handing out strips of rags. That way I could keep an eye on her and make sure she kept the job.

I tried to find out what was wrong with Malka, what had happened to bring her to this state of mind. But she stayed silent. By then I had learned that sometimes people just ended up this way, resigned to hopelessness. For them, survival had lost meaning because life had lost meaning. All joy was gone. I accepted this. The bleak grayness that permeated life in the ghetto was infectious and difficult to ward off. I guessed that Malka had lost all her family and, like so many, was alone and morose. I never knew for sure. It was always bad when people got to this point. Our group tried to protect her by encouraging her to continue coming to work. Within a few weeks though, she just stopped showing up. I don't know what happened to her.

The other teens in my group told me they enjoyed working with me as their *instruktorka*. Once, they even surprised me with a box wrapped in paper, a gift. A wrapped gift was the most unusual thing I could imagine. I eagerly unwrapped and opened the box. Inside was a beautiful silver brooch with a design of the ghetto printed on it. Inscribed on the rear of the brooch along with the day and the year, was "For our beloved *instruktorka*, Marysia." With the brooch, they gave me a little poem by one of the girls who I would later see from a distance at Auschwitz looking very pale with a rag covering her neck. I would have no chance to run over to talk to her and would never see again after that.

As they pinned the brooch on me, I was terribly moved and excited. At the time, my shift started at five in the morning, then another *Instruktorka* would take over the same group and I would work on something on my own, then go home. So the group had two *instruktorkas*. The other *instruktorka* wasn't given a gift, which made me that much more touched and honored. To me, the gift was a symbol of our mutual understanding as teenagers, recognition that I tried my best to make Klugman's a nice environment for them. I was easy going, overlooked things, and held to the notion that nothing was ever so bad that it couldn't be fixed.

The next day though, Klugman called all the *instruktorkas* into the office for a meeting. Klugman seemed old to me at the time even though he was probably only fifty. He was of average height and had a hurried sense about him. Before the war he had some professional experience that qualified him to be director of the rug workshop. I never knew what it was. Klugman's meetings were not regular things. We gathered in the office and listened to Klugman talk about how the production should be increased and how the quality of the work has been suffering. He said that the life of the shop depended on producing quality work on time. Many of the rugs were imperfect and therefore being sent back by their German recipients. At the end of the meeting we all agreed to give more attention to making sure the rugs were perfect.

"Marysia, you stay," Klugman told me as we were walking away, "I would like to speak with you privately." I didn't know what he wanted, but it couldn't be anything good.

"Listen Marysia, I know you are trying, but you have to try harder.

The work of the teenagers is very badly finished. Most of the edges develop holes and the rugs are being sent back. If the work keeps getting sent back, everybody will be sent home," he said.

"Don't' worry," I said quickly. "I'm going to personally check and double check and see that everything should be alright." And I truly thought it was going to be okay.

When I returned to the work group, they noticed that my brooch was missing. I had had it on when I went into the office but now it was gone. The others were devastated and so was I. Immediately we all fanned out to search for the brooch. We checked the office, we checked outside, all over the shop. It was nowhere to be found. Some of the children put up notices alerting everybody that if anyone finds the brooch, it should be returned to me, Marysia Gertler. But it never was returned and I never found it.

I was heartbroken. My biggest treasure had been lost and losing it was made more painful because I knew how much the other children had to give up to make the brooch—money they could have used for their rations. On top of it, I had to tell them the bad news that Klugman wanted our rugs to be finished better or else they would be sent home. I told them not to worry and that we should all pull together to help each other. I also told them that I would be helping everybody. We redoubled our efforts and worked long hours to make the rugs correctly. I was so proud to have such a wonderful group.

Two days later, I came into work and all the kids were gone. At first I thought maybe another *instruktorka* had them. But I checked with other *instruktorkas* and they didn't know where they were. Klugman's promise came true. I felt so bad I cried my heart out. I don't know what happened to them, if they found another place to work, if they were sent out of the ghetto or deported, or if they just stayed at home. They had become my friends and I missed them badly.

After this, I was reassigned another group. This time it was mostly young adults and middle-aged people. One day, a few new ladies showed up looking for a job. Though she looked pale and in poor health, I immediately recognized my grammar school teacher, Mrs. Wexler, among the new ladies. I nearly fainted. Pretending to be as grown up as possible, I asked her name. Without recognizing me, she told me. In her presence I felt bashful, like I was a child back in school. It was an awkward role reversal that I ended up teaching her how to make rugs. It was even more awkward and embarrassing that she wasn't very good at it. She tried very hard to be proficient but ended up not coming back.

I worked at Klugman's from roughly 1940 until a few months before the liquidation of the ghetto in 1944. During that time I watched hundreds of people come in and out of that shop and my life. I remember a group of Czech girls coming to work after they were relocated to the ghetto. They still looked healthy, had rosy cheeks and nourished bodies. They had fresh, nice things with them and wore new clothes. I remember thinking, "I can't believe you have the most beautiful things." But the Czech girls, like others who hadn't been in the ghetto for long, couldn't take the conditions and died quickly or were deported.

Over these years, people became too weak for work and gradually stopped showing up. Near the end of my time in the ghetto, there seemed to be a change in the general attitude and atmosphere. The work, which at one time we considered the only path to enduring in the ghetto and perhaps staying alive, stopped being important. We had seen that you could be deported regardless of your work status. Nor did your work gain you any greater access to better food. The starvation, the physical deterioration and mental exhaustion took their toll. Food stopped coming in as regularly. Families had been devastated. People were at the limit of their endurance. It was hard to sustain any kind of productive enterprise. Finally, Klugman's was closed and I couldn't work if I wanted to. Not long after, the ghetto would be emptied.

Chapter 9

By 1944, the Germans seemed to be growing desperate. Rumors began to fly that the Russians were closing in on the city. The local Polish and *Volksdeutsch*, together with the German families of SS men and army officers, were leaving the area. You could see them from the pedestrian overpasses, traveling down the Aryan streets, Zgierska and Limanowskiego, walking with bundles or driving in wagons. As this was happening, there was a massive push to empty the ghetto. Consequently, raids became more frequent. Sometimes people were just grabbed haphazardly off the street and sent out without warning. It was a miracle that Mother, Etka, Ethel, Icek and I were still together. We had five in our family. Many people didn't have any. Our luck wouldn't last much longer. The order came that all single people with names different from their families were to report for deportation. Another quota had to be met.

Ethel's last name was Dancygier. Ours was Gertler. She had been registered as Dancygier and there was no way to hide it now. It wasn't long before the Jewish police showed up at our door. They took her. There was nothing anybody could do. She looked so helpless but at the same time so much older than her years, like she knew where she was going and what was going to happen and had resigned herself to it. It made me sick that she would have to be alone and I prayed that she would be okay. I had a soft little velvet jacket, one of my last possessions, and I gave it to Ethel saying only, "Take it. Maybe you're going to need it." She took it from me and put it on.

But Mother refused to let Ethel go without a fight. In one last attempt to save her, Mother went searching for David Gertler to see if she could win an exemption for Ethel. She wasn't sure at all if she was going to succeed, but she had to try. Nothing stopped her when it came to her family. At Gertler's house, she found only his wife who said he had disappeared. She had no news of where he was beyond the fact that he had been gone some time. It was too late. That was the last day I saw or heard from Ethel. The girl who had become a sister to me, my cousin, my dear and loyal friend, Ethel Dancygier was transported to Auschwitz where she was killed.

On another occasion, while walking home Mother was caught on the street in one of the surprise raids. They lined up all the people in sight and prepared to march them to Charnieckiego, a prison that was used as a holding depot for people who were to be loaded onto rail cars at Radogoszcz train station for transport. While in line, Mother realized what was going on and surreptitiously moved backwards in the line until she reached the last position. She was buying herself time to think, to find a way to escape. Finally she saw her chance in the open doorway of a nearby home. When nobody was looking, she made a mad dash for the doorway and disappeared inside.

Looking around, she saw that nobody was there. Most of the furnishings and some other belongings remained and had not yet been appropriated for use elsewhere. Mother found a closet and closed herself in to hide. She crouched down and pulled clothing on top of her until she was well concealed by the pile. She knew that they would be searching from unlocked house to unlocked house. By now, we all knew the protocol. We had memorized every step. It was a hunting game for the Germans. We were the prey. They would enter a house, flush everybody out, then leave the house, double-locking it behind them as a sign that the place had been searched and cleared. Mother heard the familiar refrain, "Jüde, come out or you will be shot!" She heard the guards rummaging around through the apartment house, kicking things over, opening doors.

The guards came closer and stopped outside her hiding place. They flung the doors wide. Mother lay absolutely still. The guards were cursing and started to stick their bayonets into the pile of clothes. Mother kept as still and silent as a corpse. With no screaming, no blood on their bayonets and nobody anywhere else in the house, the guards exited. They locked the windows and doors. Mother let some time pass and then crept out of the closet. It was getting late. The streets were deserted and night was falling. She went to the door to leave but it was locked from the outside. She was trapped.

We didn't know where Mother was or what had happened. It was after the curfew and though in those days people were moving from hiding place to hiding place under cover of darkness, it wasn't like Mother to chance being out at night. She was supposed to be home already. We were worried sick. We had heard about the raids and were sure that she'd been caught. Right then and there, Etka, Icek, and I decided that we would march over to the precinct and volunteer for deportation just to try to be with Mother. But then, out of the blue, in walked Mother. Surprised, we all cried out for her.

She was overwhelmed with emotion. She told us what had happened with the blockade and the closet and the bayonets and getting locked inside the house. She said she knew she couldn't come out until the hunting was over, so when enough time had passed, she waited, watching out the window for a passerby. Finally, she saw an orderly patrolling the street, one of the only people who had special permission to walk the streets at that hour. She knocked on the window and called out for him to open the door. He did, and that is how she escaped and came home.

This was 1944, the beginning of the liquidation of the ghetto. Still being told that we were being moved to labor camps, we were asked to "volunteer" for deportation. But nobody trusted what we were told. They couldn't fool us. We remained somewhat ignorant of where exactly the deported people were being sent, but we knew that the Germans wouldn't tell us anything close to the truth. Plus there were the rumors of the Russian army's approach and the sight of the local Aryan population fleeing which made it known that, wherever we were asked to go, it was surely away from the Russian advance and our potential liberation.

Rumkowski and Biebow put out order after order for people to volunteer. Most of us thought that if we could just hide a little longer, the Russians would arrive and we would be free. But the Germans turned up the pressure. They halted food rations to starve people out of hiding. They tried everything and when it didn't work, they used more force.

I lived in constant fear that summer. Sometimes I fooled myself by thinking that the deportees were actually being sent to work camps. Maybe Rumkowski's "refuge through work" would continue in those camps. Starvation was affecting my thinking. I had become inconsolable but had not lost hope. Mother would remind us to keep faith in God and believe that we would survive. She said that the Russians were pushing forward and that we would soon be discovered. I told her that I had heard rumors that the Russians would rape us, shoot us, drop bombs on us or put us in prisons. She said it wasn't true.

The SS raided the street where we lived once again. The soldiers were more menacing and angrier now. They were frustrated that the war was going badly and that people weren't reporting as they were ordered to do. We certainly weren't going to volunteer ourselves. Even after our rations were cut off, we didn't report. After all, the Germans were losing. Their sick war was ending. Why should we do anything to comply with them? But this time hiding wouldn't work. There would be no escaping their hunt. They went methodically from one house to the next. They emptied out Zydowska 25 and brought us to Charnieckiego to await transport.

At Charnieckiego, Mother was determined to hold out and stay off the transports as long as possible. She watched for a way out. She always believed that there had to be a way out. She wouldn't give in, especially knowing what the Germans wanted to do in spite of what they were telling us. Finally, she saw that the guy who was in charge had looked away and was busy with something. One by one, she sneaked us out of there.

Our escape was successful and we were free for the moment, but we had no place to go. There were soldiers and raids everywhere and no way to hide. We couldn't go back to our apartment because it had been emptied out and locked. We rushed from side street to side street, hugging building walls as we made our way to an apartment building where some people Mother knew had been hiding out. Thus far they had evaded the raids. We arrived at the building and hurried inside.

At first, we didn't see anybody, but then one of the men who Mother knew came out of a door. They exchanged some words and he pointed us upstairs. Mother said thank you and led us up to the third floor. The apartment was large for the ghetto. Everything looked normal about it. There was a double closet in one of the rooms that we decided would be our main place to hide. We stayed in the apartment about two weeks, never venturing out except one night when Mother snuck out to look for food and came back with a moldy loaf of bread. She said she found it in one of the empty apartments. We were starving and had to eat it.

We would hear what seemed like a constant marching of soldiers passing outside the window. Every time, we ducked down out of sight and prayed that they would pass us. Then one night, we heard the familiar loud pounding on a neighbor's door. They had come for the group that Mother knew, the people hiding in the apartment on the first floor.

We rushed into our double closet and closed the door tightly behind us. Inside, it was dark and claustrophobic, but we all fit by scrunching up against the walls. We sat as silent as ghosts, hoping that there was still a chance that the Germans wouldn't search the rest of the building. But they did, stomping between floors, rummaging through all possible hiding places, emptying out the entire building.

I heard their loud boots stomping up the stairs to our floor. I looked at Mother's face, then Etka's. In the shadows and thin cracks of light I could see that, despite their fear, they were trying to remain still as statues. As the Germans continued searching they shouted, "Get out of your hiding places! We know you are here!" I pushed a little further back into a corner of the closet. I was jittery. My hands were shaking and wouldn't stop. I didn't want to make a noise so I sat down and hugged my knees, staring at my feet. I looked up briefly at Icek. He looked back at me. There was a combination of fear and detachment in his eyes. It looked like his mind was absent and somewhere far from here, but then he reached down and touched my shoulder reassuringly.

The Germans were in our apartment now, stomping closer, turning over chairs and tables. Then with a sudden rush of light, the closet doors were flung open. I looked up to see a big, shadowy silhouette, another mercenary of death in a metal helmet and shoulder-swung submachine gun. The soldier hardly reacted to us. He didn't shout. He didn't provoke. He didn't draw his weapon to shoot. He just stood there emotionless, and matter-of-factly spoke. "Get out *verflüchte Jüde.* Do you want to be shot?" We did as he ordered.

It was overcast and hot outside when they lined us up on the street. We climbed into a wagon with about twenty other people from different parts of the ghetto, others who had tried to evade by hiding. As we moved again to Charnieckiego to be held for transport, I looked at the people around me. Their faces were all worried, despondent. There was no time for anything other than being concerned with each other. I hardly noticed the buildings, vacant and dead, passing in a slow blur of broken and shuttered windows.

We stayed overnight at Charnieckiego. It was uncomfortable and unusually cold. It was the last place we stayed in the ghetto. The next morning we were loaded onto the tramway and taken to the train station where a train with people already on it was waiting. It was the first time we were allowed to be on the tramway in years. We were each given one portion of bread and then shoved into a boxcar until it was crammed full with bodies.

Not knowing where we were heading or how long it would take, standing pinned shoulder to shoulder with others, Etka and I grew panicky. Icek kept very quiet, not questioning, not saying a word. Icek's withdrawal had started to concern us but we were all too hungry and weak to do anything about it. Too many things were happening. We had been on the run for weeks, hiding, trying to escape the burning fire of the Nazi's pursuit. There was no exit or escape, but we clung to the little faith we had left, hoping to overcome, to survive.

Mother tried to calm us down and took our bread from us to save it for when we arrived at our new "place of work." She asked if we wanted a piece of bread before the train started moving. Etka and I wanted to wait. Icek said "yes" and ate his portion ravenously. This made us feel better, like he was okay because he still wanted to eat. Mother tried to reassure us the way she always did. She said we would be okay. I wanted to believe her. Somewhere deep down I knew that I had to believe her if I was going to survive.

I had entered the ghetto at fourteen and was leaving at eighteen going on nineteen. We had grown up a lot in that time. But how we changed couldn't be measured in years. There were no smiling eyes, just emptiness and seriousness. We looked at life differently, had been marked in unseen ways with scars underneath the skin. Our behavior, our thinking–just emptiness and seriousness. Seventy thousand Jews were deported that summer–the last of us to be sent out before the ghetto was officially shutdown and closed. Rumkowski was eventually sent out as well. He left the ghetto with the last transport when, after being unable to get an exception for his brother, he decided to join him. Rumkowski, his wife, his adopted son, and his brother were all sent to Auschwitz. Initially we had heard that he went to the gas chamber. Later, we learned that he was killed by a group of former Jewish inmates who had been in the Łódź ghetto. Several hundred Jews were all that remained behind in the ghetto, the last remaining to do the work of dismantling machinery and gathering goods to be sent back to the Reich.

Chapter 10

We left the Łódź ghetto sometime in late June or early July. When we were loaded onto the train, we didn't yet know that it was going to Auschwitz. They told us we were being moved to a labor camp. It was humid and late in the day when the boxcar finally started to roll away. We had been put in with Jewish people from other areas, not just Łódź. There was no air, no water, no relief, and no sunlight. The train moved painfully slowly.

We thought the Nazi's would open the doors so we could breathe; perhaps give us some water for our dry throats, but the doors weren't opened. The water didn't come. And the train never stopped. For some reason, there was salt all over the floor of these cars and it evaporated up into our mouths and nostrils, drying them out thoroughly. There wasn't much talking or even moaning and crying from the crowd in the train car. We had spent four years in the ghetto, cramped, deprived and afraid. Now, here we were, numbed by our experience, with just our clothes and our bodies remaining of all that had been plundered and destroyed.

The whole trip from Łódź to Auschwitz took a couple of hours. I was thankful it wasn't longer. The train arrived and the doors were thrown open onto a long platform where SS men and their dogs stood waiting. Behind them, I could see a sprawling complex of low buildings and Jewish men wearing flannel outfits of blue and gray stripes rushing from place to place. The atmosphere here felt awkward and uneasy. The air at this place wasn't fresh when the doors of the boxcar were opened. It was thick and stifling, muggy and hot. I remember that it smelled grotesquely sweet and I found out later that it was from the crematoria smokestacks. I didn't know at the time that I was at Auschwitz or what being there meant.

We crawled out of the railcar or jumped down to the ground below.

There were no stairs, walking planks or raised platforms to aid us. We were treated like cargo being dumped out and counted. The SS men commanded us to stand in lines. Children were immediately separated from their Mothers and put in their own line. If the Mothers held on or protested, they would be taken with the children. The SS soldiers simply spoke and pointed, "You go here. You go there."

The men were separated from the women and moved to a different section of the platform. I turned and suddenly saw Icek being shoved into a crowd of men. It happened so fast and took me by utter surprise. There was hardly a last look between us. No goodbye and no tears. I wanted to rush forward, grab him and hold on, but couldn't. Neither could Etka or Mother. Our brother, Mother's youngest son, was gone. We prayed that he would be okay but that afternoon was the last time we saw him. He was fifteen, on the verge of becoming a man. He had grown up a lot in the last few years, but in my mind, he was still the cherished eleven-year-old boy who liked to play long into the evening on the streets with the other boys. Just like that, he was gone.

Next, the SS men separated the women into a right and a left line. They went quickly over each person making their selections. We didn't know the difference between the two lines. It seemed arbitrary and superficial, subject only to the SS inspector's personal whim. But then one of the prisoners in striped pajamas who was working near us turned to face in our direction and made eye contact. He signaled us by silently, unnoticeably motioning to the right to show us that this is where we wanted to go. I was the first in my row. The SS man stepped in front of me. He checked me over quickly and pointed to the right.

Mother was behind me and next to be inspected. The SS man stopped. He hesitated and looked closely at her. Before leaving the ghetto, she had put on two coats in case we would need the extra coat for something. But now the bulk of both coats made her look unusually thick in the belly, perhaps pregnant, or perhaps the opposite, trying to hide being sickly. Seeing the guard's hesitation, she immediately threw open the coats and held their flaps wide to show she was not pregnant or sickly. She spoke resolutely to the SS man, "I am strong, young, and healthy. I can work."

He gave her one last look and sent her in my direction. I sighed briefly then watched as the guard moved on to inspect Etka. Of all of us, Etka had always had the best physical constitution. She was the strong and athletic one. Even though she too was abominably thin she still gave off the appearance of being physically able. She passed inspection and was sent to the right with us. I looked at Mother and at Etka. These selections happened quickly. There was no time to process what was happening, nor was there time nor benefit in doing anything other than burying the loss of our brother deep within us.

We were marched in rows from the unloading platform toward a brick building and forced to go inside. We were ordered to remove all of our clothes and to place them on huge piles on the floor where others before us had left theirs. We did the same with our shoes. Naked, guards led us to a different building where we stood in line for another inspection. This time it was by doctors accompanied by other SS men and women. Next, we shuffled through a room where our heads were hurriedly shaved. Finally we were ordered into an adjacent room. "Now you're going to get a shower," a guard told us.

But we never made it into the shower room. As we were entering, air raid sirens started to blare outside. The SS screamed at us to get out. We were grouped together with others already standing outside. There were hundreds of us standing there, naked, skinny, scared, skeletal, exposed. The sirens lasted for about half the day and that's how long we stood there. The Germans had rushed to find shelter or to mobilize and left us with just a few guards. I could hear the bombs going off not far away. They were being dropped from planes. I wondered if they would drop them on our camp.

I felt disgraced, humiliated and embarrassed, standing there without clothes on, my body in disrepair from years of malnutrition. I had never been naked so publicly. I had never stood face-to-face, arm-to-arm with so many naked people before. And even though we were all in the same situation, I became overwhelmed with shame and tried to cover myself with my arms. Looking at Mother and Etka, I hardly recognized them. They looked strange, awkward, alien. Their bodies were like reflections in a mirror. And in the absence of real mirrors, they were the closest things I had to a reflection. I saw in them, in the others around me, my own image. There we stood as one, a collective of heads shaved patchy and bald, bony naked bodies, pitiful, thinned, degraded.

I began to cry and asked through my tears, "Do I also look like this?"

Mother saw that I was upset and touched me reassuringly on the shoulder. She kissed me on the cheek and said, "Don't worry my child. Your hair will grow back more beautiful than ever. Trust me."

The sirens finally stopped and, still naked, we were ordered to stand in a single line to receive a bowl of soup. We were told we had to share it with four others. Mother and Etka stood ahead of me. Somehow a woman I did not know had gotten between us. The woman was the first of our four. She was ladled a bowl of soup, took a long drink and then handed it to me. I hesitated, somehow able to still conjure up disgust at the thought of how unhygienic this was. But I put the bowl to my lips, taking only a tiny, tentative sip and passing it onto the next person. After the soup, we were taken back to the pile of clothes and shoes. A few Jewish prisoners stood by the pile and indiscriminately handed out the items. We were each given one dress and one pair of shoes. I received a black dress with short sleeves that was much too big for me. Likewise, the old shoes I was handed were too big and were also full of holes. The same was true for everybody else. Nobody's clothes fit. We looked like escapees from a sanitarium.

Wearing those ill-fitting clothes, we were told to stand in lines to be registered. The oversized shoes slipped and slid uncomfortably with each step as I took my place and waited. The line moved at a steady clip, the process repeating itself over and over. A Jewish prisoner would step up to the table and a German guard would put her name in a log and give her a number. Next to the guard, another guard would tattoo that number on the prisoner's left forearm. I remember watching it, waiting for my turn. There were two people ahead of me and inexplicably, miraculously they weren't tattooed. The Germans stopped tattooing just two people before it was my turn. I never found out why, but they stopped. Instead we were given a number on a strip of cloth that we had to sew onto our dresses.

When registration was complete, we were taken to our temporary barracks where we remained for about two weeks. We did nothing for those two weeks except stand outside for many hours during long morning roll-calls, eat our meager ration of soup, and wait to find out what we would be doing, where we would be going. We continued to know nothing and stayed packed into those barracks, sleeping on the cold, hard floor planks until we were told to line up and get ready to move to another camp. I didn't know why they wanted to move us so quickly. And they didn't tell us where we would be going.

Back on the train, we were packed in more tightly, stuffed and squeezed again like animals. There were hundreds, if not thousands of us being shoved into those cattle cars. The conditions, the stench, and the crush of bodies were unbearable. We stood silently, struggling to stand and breathe with people practically climbing on top of one another to get space. Finally the doors were slid shut and the iron locking pins slammed with a clank.

These boxcars had salt on the floor again which made my dehydration unbearable. For food, we had been given half-cooked, straw-covered and sand-covered potatoes with the peels still on them. We were all starving and so ate the potatoes. Again there was no water, no air, no window, no ventilation. The only place to relieve ourselves if we couldn't hold it was right where we stood. It wasn't long after the train started moving that everyone in the car began to get the most awful stomach pangs. The raw potatoes, together with the dehydration, heat, and suffocating lack of air made people violently ill. They wretched. Vomited. People with dysentery and diarrhea had no choice but to let it go. Mother screamed in agony and folded tightly at the belly in excruciating pain. She held onto her stomach and tried to bear the pain. I'd never seen her like that. People were fainting. They were close to death, some dying, their lifeless bodies too pinned between others to slump to the floor.

It was like this for hours as the train chugged along for most of the day and into night before finally stopping. "Why was it stopping?" I thought to myself. We heard the sounds of the SS moving down the line, unlocking the cars. They unlocked our car and slid open the door. Instantly people gasped for air. Dead bodies trailed out as people stumbled out of the cars. A couple of us managed to climb out relatively calmly. Some people were ordered by the guards to get rid of the dead bodies, which were then piled up next to the rails.

It was a crisp, clear night and stars blanketed the sky. We stood in an open field adjacent to the stopped train. There were some trees in the distance and some kind of army encampment in the nearer distance at the edge of the field. It was the middle of nowhere, but oddly among the tents in the encampment, I saw what looked like Japanese or Chinese soldiers. I had no idea why they were there and in the condition I was in, it's possible that they could have been another army's soldiers. They were far away and small in the distance but they didn't look German. They didn't come near us, just stood on the side of the field by their tents.

Even though we had already been vacated, there was still boiling steam coming from the cattle cars because of the body heat trapped inside. When the guards finished letting everybody out, they informed us that we were spending the night right there in the open field. I didn't mind the lack of any form of shelter though since the night was cool and the fresh air somehow took away a bit of the terrible thirst. The grassy field and the open air refreshed my badly deteriorated body and helped me to feel momentarily alive again.

When the sun rose, the early morning air appeared gray and misty. Underneath us, dew covered the grass. Above, the sun found cracks in the cloud cover and broke through in thin shafts of bright light. It looked like it would be a sunny day, humid and hot. We were afforded but a few hours of rest before being awakened and loaded up again into the cattle car with the salted floor. My lips were dry and painfully blistered and cracked. I didn't think they could get any worse.

Mother, Etka and I stood near each other, barely speaking for the entire ride to our next destination. We still didn't know where we were being taken or how much longer we would have to be on the train. I was severely dehydrated and thirsty. The heat in the car burrowed under my skin and dried out every part of me. My body felt faint and weak. Mother saw me in this condition and commented that I looked sickly pale. But she couldn't do anything except hope I would be okay and pray that I held on for the remainder of the ride. It took most of the next day to get to what ended up being the camps at Stutthof. When the train finally arrived, I was burning up with fever and morbidly ill.

Chapter 11

Stutthof was in the Gdansk region close to the Baltic Sea–the north of what was then the eastern part of the Reich, but just a few years before had been Poland. We were assigned to a barracks that was already crowded with people. Some of us asked the people, "Where would be sleeping?" and were told, "Right here, on the wooden floor." In the barracks each one of us received a blanket, a dish, and a bowl to be used for food. But people used those bowls for anything, including pillows.

My fever had become progressively worse. At midnight, my skin was hotter than fire and I had a splitting headache. Sleep was impossible. The floorboards beneath me pierced and dug into my flesh. Mother saw me tossing relentlessly. She put her hand to my cheek and neck and realized I needed help immediately. There was a young Jewish woman in charge of the barracks named Rozka, also from Poland. Mother told her that I was very sick and needed to get help. Rozka sent me to the small camp hospital because that's what she had been ordered to do with the sick.

I checked in and was given a pill. They put me on the top bed of a three-tiered bunk. There was no mattress but I had more space to move here. The Jewish nurse told me that I would be okay and to rest. She told me that every week or two the SS would show up to remove the sick people. But they had just come two days earlier so I had a few days to get well. Just to be safe, she said I would likely be released in three days. I listened carefully to her and fell into a deep sleep. The next day, my fever decreased and I felt slightly better. Neither Mother nor Etka could come see me that day. I don't know what they were doing. Most likely they were consigned to some labor. The third day came and I waited for my release, but even though my fever was gone and I felt well, it didn't happen. I didn't mind staying though, and thought it better that I be fully recovered and able to work when I got out.

I tried to sleep but woke up from the sounds of onrushing footsteps and other noises. It was the SS troops. Unexpected. They were early. They had stormed in, kicked out the nurses and were forcing all the sick people outside. Scared and confused, I didn't know what to do. I had no escape so I lay there, silently and still on my upper bunk, while the SS went from bunk to bunk emptying out the infirmary. Then all the action abruptly stopped. The SS had gone and the room was quiet. I was still there. They missed my bunk. They overlooked me, were somehow blinded. I was the only one left in the hospital. I wasn't sure if they were going to come back in, so I remained quiet and unmoving.

In the barracks, Mother and Etka heard that the hospital had been emptied out. They also heard that the people were taken straight to the crematorium to be burned alive. Mother couldn't believe it. Without a moment's hesitation, she headed to the hospital to see for herself. Near the hospital, there was a section of the camp for the *Roma*, the gypsies. They blocked Mother's path to the hospital. They told her that the Nazi's had removed all the patients. They told her not to go inside, warning that there was still a danger the SS would return. Mother didn't listen and maneuvered around them to the hospital entrance.

Inside, she found the hospital deserted. There wasn't a single person left on the beds. Regardless, she walked through the room, checking bunks and calling out my name. "Mashéle! Mashéle!" I could hear her but was too frightened to answer right away. Then in a quiet voice, I managed, "Mother, I am here."

Mother ran over to my bunk. She helped me down and put her arms around me. Showering me with kisses, she thanked God over and over that I was saved and took me with her back to the barracks. We passed the gypsies who couldn't believe that I had survived the sweep. We got to the barrack and people there also couldn't believe it. Etka hugged me. They were all happy to see me alive and well.

Each day at Stutthof started the same way with us waking well before dawn and getting in place for a roll call. We lined up outside the barracks in the cold and dark, standing in the frozen air without socks, sweaters, or coats. My only possession was my one black dress and holey shoes. I slept, walked and lived in them. For the roll calls, everyone from all the barracks and blockhouses at Stutthof were ordered out and counted at the same time. Often, due to a miscount, we had to be counted numerous times. This routine would take hours and hours and then happen a second time in the evening. We had to stand for the entire count. After the count, we were given negligible rations of bread and watery soup.

At one morning's roll call, in the distance I saw Fela Adlic, one of my friends from the ghetto and fellow *instruktorka* at Klugman's. I waved to her and we made our way toward each other. She was sick and was heading for the camp hospital. She was wearing two sweaters and wanted to give me one. But I wouldn't take it. I told her that I could be sent out to work or something worse just as easily and suddenly as she could. If I were sent out, she would be without a second sweater. So she kept the sweater. That was the last we saw of each other.

I also saw another girlfriend I knew from the ghetto, Rysia. She was in our barrack, alive but very weak and nearing death. News came that a *Stubenaelteste* from another barracks wanted her portrait painted and asked if there were any artists who could do it. Rysia was a talented artist and could do it. It would mean great things for her like more food, perhaps better treatment. But she was too weak to stand the immense cold outside. I offered her some stockings I had so that she could bear the cold, but she simply didn't have the strength. She eventually died.

After about a month of living in one barrack we were transferred to a much larger one. There were hundreds more people in this place and less space for each person. We were packed in more tightly than sardines and could hardly move. When we lay down to sleep, bodies were butted so close to one another that limbs would inevitably get tangled or crossed. The one in charge of this barrack was an awful, cruel woman named Basia. She was Czech and had a twin whose name I don't recall. The two of them were volunteers with the SS.

There was a woman named Plywacka in our block who was from Poland. She was very tall and couldn't find a place for her long legs to stretch out at night. Nobody wanted to lie in her area because her legs and feet would overflow onto you. You would spend all night pushing her feet away only to have them pushed back by somebody else. I recall one night when her legs landed on me. They were bulky and heavy. My fragile frame could hardly bear the pressure but I stayed quiet and let them be. She had no control over how tall she was. I felt sorry for her even though I was hurting and completely unable to move or shift under the weight of those long legs. I simply adjusted the shoes under my head that I was using as a pillow and tried to make it work so that I could sleep. In the morning, my pillow switched roles to become my shoes once more, still flimsy, full of holes and by now held together only with a string.

It was the end of 1944 and the weather was getting much colder. The floor where we slept became colder too. In this barrack, a thin layer of gravel covered the floor. When I lay on it, the small stones would stick into my flesh, becoming embedded and leaving marks, tiny bruises and other wounds. There were windows on either side of the barrack that were always open. Usually windows were closed and locked and I don't remember why these windows were open but when it rained, water poured in through them and pooled on the floor. When it snowed, the snow would float in, pile up and then melt. We had to lie in those pools of water and snow. Our bodies were already skin and bones, sick with hunger and disease, hardly able to keep our blood warm enough.

The floor where I slept was always damp, there were no facilities for washing, and we would get pieces of bread less frequently. The soup was watery and good for nothing. Going to the bathroom was difficult because there were no walls between the toilets. The room was just one long, open latrine. Frequently, I would have to wait until the whole place emptied out before I was comfortable enough to go. But the hardest thing was the roll calls, the endless hours and hours of standing up hungry and tired in the cold and wet while waiting to be counted.

I got sick again. My body had grown terribly weak. I had lice all over my clothes and in my hair. My body was in a dire state, my flesh had deep cuts and red welts and my bones were constantly sore from sleeping on the gravel floor. I learned not to complain and to live with it. But my illness became so bad that one morning I wasn't able to stand up for roll call. I hardly remember what happened but Mother and Etka somehow managed to carry me out just before our barrack was counted. Then after I was counted, they brought me back in and hid me until the count for the whole camp was over. They prayed and hoped that there wouldn't have to be a recount. I could never have remained standing for the lengthy process. The SS would have spotted me struggling and falling to the ground and recognized me as sick. Sick people were taken straight to the crematoria.

A woman named Frida, a Jewish girl from France, had orders to remove any person suspected of contagion. She kept a list of people recommended for the infirmary. But most of the people who were reported and sent would not come back. Frida had been a nurse before the war. She was a good person charged with an awful duty. I had grown delirious with fever and was in a lot of pain. Frida came over and took my temperature. It was dangerously high. Frida was torn. She had to put me on the list. She said I was going to die if I didn't get help, but I would also die if I did get help. Mother knew that if Frida put me on the list, it wouldn't be the infirmary I was going to. She pleaded with Frida, asking her to wait, to give me just a few more days to come out of it. She said, "If my daughter has to die, at least she will be here with me and I will be at peace knowing what has happened to her. I cannot forgive myself otherwise."

Frida reluctantly agreed. She told Mother again how dire my condition was. Mother nodded and said she understood and would pray for me. That night I had a vision. A fire was raging, flames hovering just above me, and then words were spoken by a stern voice. I was told to shift my eyes to the left. I obeyed and saw a wall made of large stone blocks the way certain ancient walls were made. The stones were gray and chalky in appearance and stretched higher and wider than my eyes could see. I traced the lines between the stones down to where the wall met the ground. There, the stones cracked and crumbled a little. When I woke up and opened my eyes, the fever had broken and I felt better. Mother's prayers were answered. Frida was relieved to know that she didn't have to report me. God clothed me with robes of mercy and healed me with his love. His holiness awakened me to life again.

In the beginning at Stutthof, things were still relatively organized and controlled. Work wasn't plentiful, but it was possible to be selected for some task and sent out to spend the day doing it. Overall, I wasn't assigned much work at Stutthof. When I did work, it was usually digging potatoes with Mother and Etka. I was ill much of the time, so Mother and Etka did not want me to go dig potatoes with them, but one day I *did* go. Somehow I had gotten my hands on a shawl and I wore it to work. At the end of the day, I stuck one potato under the shawl and tried to smuggle it into the barracks. But a female guard stopped and inspected me. She found my hidden potato and took it. Then she punched me square in the face and sent me away. I did not volunteer for work after that.

Mother regularly woke up each morning at around three or four in order to try to get the job peeling potatoes and chopping vegetables. She did this because she was sometimes able to sneak a few potatoes back to the barrack and exchange them for some soup with the *Stubenaelteste*, the one in charge of the barracks, or permission to use her little stove to cook the potatoes. Bringing back the potatoes was always taking a big risk. But Mother didn't care. We were starving and she wanted us to eat.

There was a girl named Luba in our barrack who had just returned from a work detail outside the camp. She looked fresher and healthier than the rest of us. Some time before we arrived, she had been "rented" to a local farm where she lived and worked for the harvest season. She told us that the work was difficult but that she was fed one solid meal a day and was able to sleep in a barn. She didn't mind sleeping in the barn or doing the farm work and wished that she could still be there. When she departed, the farmer gave her a piece of bread, some onions and a bar of soap. She was wearing both a sweater and a coat when she returned.

One day, the weather was nasty—cold, sleeting, and freezing. But Mother was undeterred and wanted to get work. She asked Luba if she could borrow her coat for the day in exchange for any potatoes she was able to sneak back. Luba was delighted to help and gave Mother the coat. It had huge pockets and a wonderful double lining. Mother thought it was perfect. She could hide more potatoes and feed more people. The coat would make it hard to detect the hidden food.

Mother was selected for work that day and toward the end of the day filled her pockets with potatoes, stuffing some in the coat's lining. The workers were lined up and readied for escort back to our block when SS guards with dogs showed up. With the dogs barking madly, they started shouting orders to people to empty their pockets and throw everything onto the ground at their feet. The SS guards walked the line of workers threatening that they were going to sic the dogs on them. We knew by then that if released, the dogs would go straight for your throat, scratching and biting at flesh and clothing until the blood poured from your neck.

Frightened, the workers hurried to throw out everything they had in their pockets. With each toss, the SS guard would let the dog loose on the person. The dog would tear at the person's clothing and skin and then be pulled back. But Mother didn't budge. She took nothing out of her pockets and waited for the SS and their dogs to leave. They did and all the women returned to the barracks. We already knew what had happened by the time they got back. We were happy they were all alive and unharmed but were disheartened because we had started to count on the potatoes they would bring back. Then Mother unexpectedly began to empty Luba's coat. She revealed more potatoes than we had seen in a long time. She convinced the one in charge to share in the feast and was allowed to cook them on the little stove. Everybody got a little bit that night. Mother never went back to work after this.

Transports with new arrivals came into camp daily. The new arrivals were mostly Hungarians. To our surprise, their hair wasn't shaved, their clothes fit well and seemed to be their own, and their faces were more full and robust-looking. They must have come directly from their homes and weren't at all used to being in the camps like we were. Lice and disease quickly and mercilessly ravaged their bodies. They couldn't stand the hunger and filth. At night, their screams and cries were nonstop. They died in the hundreds within weeks of their arrival. If they complained, they were shot or sent to the crematoria.

I never thought that such conditions like those I experienced first in the ghetto, then at Auschwitz, then at Stutthof, could exist or that they could get progressively worse. We went from one state of inhuman conditions to a further state of inhuman conditions. It was like going from one level of hell to a deeper level of hell. The stench, the crowding, the disease, the hunger, the cold was unbearable, but I kept the challenge of survival foremost in my mind and did my best to endure.

People started dying more frequently; the death toll went up daily. Every night we lay shoulder-to-shoulder with the dead and dying. We listened to the sobs and the earnest prayers to God and other mutterings for somebody to help, somebody to stay close. The dying people always wanted somebody to be there with them, to hold them as they went. They were scared. Each morning there were new dead bodies. Mother and Etka and others would take them outside or, after the doors were locked, place them in the rear of the barracks. As the days passed, those of us still alive grew ever more withdrawn. The pain and suffering continued on its endless path and it was like we had given up on words. Talking could do nothing. Our bodies had been tortured by hunger and disease, deprived to their very limits. With this torture, more and more people began to lose their minds.

There was a young woman I slept next to. She was one of those people touching on madness. She told me she was married to a wonderful young man, a dentist, who put in gold teeth for her. She said she loved him more than anything. They had been married for a year and were planning to start a family. They had a bright future planned. She spoke about him as if he were there with her even though he was not. One night, as the young woman was telling me about her husband the dentist, she suddenly started shivering wildly. She said, "I feel so cold and alone," and then the shivering stopped. She died. I wondered if she was telling me about the gold teeth so that I could salvage the gold, but I wouldn't think of it.

We were transferred to a third barrack on a block called the 31st block. It was known as the worst in the camp. Illness, hallucination-inducing fever, and death were rampant. Not even the Germans wanted to come near this place. It was no surprise when typhus took hold. It had already taken hold of the entire camp and people were suffering unimaginable pain. It was the middle of winter. Snow was lining the frozen ground of our barracks. Our bodies were ridden with lice and crowded together. The disease spread like wildfire from person to person and the order came to quarantine our block. We couldn't leave and nobody outside could come in. Food and water distribution was halted. People died in the hundreds and were left to lie where they died. Nobody came anymore to remove the dead in order to burn or bury them. Outside and inside the barracks, it became an open graveyard of corpses.

We lived in this open graveyard for months. It got so that the only way you could tell the difference between the living and the dead was that the living moved occasionally. But the living were also the dying. All of us who had been struck with the infectious disease were feverish and delirious. We had nothing to warm us and shivered constantly from the cold. There was madness in people's eyes and incoherent muttering all around. Often, somebody would reach up, breathe deeply and beg, "Please give me some water."

The misery of that time took a total and complete effect on our lives. In this extreme absence of food, I began to long for the watery soup I had earlier so despised. My only solace was that, in quarantine, there were no daily counts, no pistol shots at people. There was still, though, always the threat that maybe they would come eliminate the typhus problem by eliminating us. Etka had always been resilient in the midst of these conditions. But one morning after waking, she was smiling and unusually excited. She seemed delusional and Mother and I thought she had lost her mind.

Mother asked, "Etka, why are you smiling? What could you be happy about?"

Etka said, "Listen to me, I saw Father sitting on a white horse that was slung with huge packs filled with all kinds of food. I have never seen so much food before in my life. He gave me the food and I ate and ate and ate until I couldn't eat anymore."

"Etka, there is nobody here on a white horse," Mother said.

But she continued, "Then Dad told me not to worry because we would be okay."

It was her dream that had given her joy enough to smile. Her fever broke that day. To her, our Father really was there, really did visit. He brought her food and talked with her. You couldn't convince her otherwise. She held onto that dream and wasn't hungry for a long time afterwards.

Weeks passed and conditions grew ever more appalling. The air smelled of decaying bodies and dried urine. The starvation worsened. Our bodies became skin and bones continually ravaged by lice that no longer pretended to hide and now crawled openly all over us—little black specks jumping across clothes, blanketing the floor. I tried desperately to disconnect, to separate myself from my body so that I could separate from the pain and suffering. But my eyes never let me disconnect. If I turned to one side, there was the misery and suffering. If I turned to another side, there it was too. I felt forgotten, disembodied, like an observer watching my own death. I was trapped between life and death and the life part had the more difficult burden. Death would have been kinder at that point. "Is life better than death?" I asked myself. I battled back and forth with life and with death until I became obsessed with holding onto life until its very last breath was taken away from me. As long as I stayed alive, there was promise; death meant silence.

Mother knew that if she didn't do something we would all die like the others dying among us. Though weak and feverish, she managed to crawl to a closed window and push it open a little. The cold air rushed in. She reached out and grabbed a handful of snow. It was falling mercifully and filled up her tiny palm. She brought the snow in and put it to her burning lips. Then she reached out for more snow, which she brought around to others in the barrack and put gently to their lips, cooling the ever-present burning.

Mother wanted to get outside the barrack. She knew she had to do something for her own and for her children's sake. But because of the quarantine, the door had been locked. So Mother tried to open the window wide, but it too was jammed. Watching her was like watching a shadow. Just bones, her body was barely visible. She hit on the window and managed to knock it open. Then, unafraid and with all her strength, she managed to climb out. She went around to the door and forced it open. She came back and retrieved her bowl. With her bowl in hand, she made her way outside in the snow to a nearby faucet. She filled the bowl with water and started to make her way back when a German supervisor, a female SS, stopped her.

The SS woman yelled, "*Die verflüchte Jüde!* What are you doing outside?"

Mother didn't respond. She just stood still while the supervisor picked up a stone and threw it. It struck Mother square on the front-side of the forehead and she fell to the ground, dropping the bowl. The supervisor watched her fall and then abruptly left. Blood was gushing from Mother's head as she rose up and went back to the faucet. She filled the bowl with water and dropped suddenly to her knees, crawling back to the barrack entrance. Seeing her enter, bloody and injured, I cried bitterly. Mother stayed strong and made her way over to me to give me two spoonfuls of water like it was medicine.

"I would rather have you give me poison than to have to watch you suffer that way," I told her. But she didn't want to hear it. The point was that we had water. As I spoke, she was already moving on to my sister, giving her a few spoonfuls of water. She continued down the line of people, spooning out tiny pools of water to every thirsty mouth.

Hardly a body was left alive in that dark, rotting space. The starvation prevailed. The graveyard of fallen bodies around us remained. But it wasn't our time to die. God breathed new life into us. Miraculously, Etka, Mother and I recovered from the illness. Mother summoned what was left of her strength and exited the barrack, telling us she would be back soon. She was headed to another barrack in a block not too far away and moved with much difficulty. She would fall then get up and walk, fall then get up and walk. I watched her go from the doorway until she disappeared around a bend. She reached the other barrack and upon entering, collapsed. The women inside the barrack rushed to her aid. They held her up and sat her down in a chair. She was barely able to keep her head up. Her chin sank to her chest. A woman named Regina came near. When Mother looked up, they recognized each other.

Regina had lived in the Łódź ghetto. She had some family in the apartment next door to ours and often came to visit them. Regina was excited to see Mother but worried about her weakened state. She immediately brought Mother some water and helped her to drink.

"Cypa, what is happening?" she asked.

Mother told her everything: that there was practically nobody left alive in our barrack, that Etka and I were alive and waiting for her to return, that those remaining alive would not stay that way for long. Regina told Mother that there was nobody left in charge of her barrack anymore so she had taken the position. Regina gathered two women and returned to us with a wagon that had been used to haul garbage. They came back to help us get out of the open graveyard. They entered, lifted us under our arms, and carried us out. I had not been outside for months. The winter air was bitterly refreshing. Upon feeling it, a crisp bolt of energy rushed through my body, awakening me to life again. I took as deep a breath as my lungs would allow.

We scrambled into the wagon. Regina and the two women began to pull us toward their barrack. I watched the camp pass as we went and was horrified by what I saw: more dead bodies, just skin and skeleton, masses of twisted gaping faces, wide, screaming eyes, bony elbows and knees broken, tossed onto each other until you could barely make out where one body stopped and the other started. Skin pale yellow and brown, ravaged by unhealed wounds and decay, they rose up like a sick sculpture, their souls banded together to ascend and be received by the Almighty. They were still, motionless, silent, unmarked, unnamed, unknown. I asked then of death what is death, and death was silent and motionless.

There was a blanket of deep winter white snow on the ground and covering some of the frozen bodies. Cold, dry, hungry and weak, we arrived at Regina's barrack. My gums were in terrible pain and my teeth were shifting back and forth as I unconsciously ground them against each other. Etka too was grinding her teeth. Regina looked at us in this miserable state and said "I'll try all I can to help you."

She brought us inside and sat us down on an empty bunk. This barrack was much warmer and smaller. Regina told us to lie down and said she would go to find something to help us. I could barely swallow and everything in my body hurt when I lay back on the hard bed-boards. I fell asleep briefly and when I awoke Regina was standing near, waiting with some purple antiseptic water. She gave it to us and told us to gargle a few times a day saying that it would help our gums. The next day, she brought us some bread that had been soaked in hot water to make it easier to swallow. She also found some blankets for us to use to cover up and stay warm. She was like an angel bringing us blessings and gifts from heaven. I thanked God and gradually started to feel better.

We stayed in this barrack for the rest of our time at Stutthof. Eventually, the weather started to warm up, though it was still cold, and the camp started to be emptied. The Germans came around ordering, "All who can walk or are strong must go." Those who felt they could go were transported to other camps at Gdansk or Gdynia. Those who were weak stayed behind. We were in the group that stayed behind. Soon, we started to hear mumblings that the Germans were losing the war, that the camp was being emptied in order to flee the approaching Russians.

Chapter 12

Because the ones in charge of the barracks had all fled, there was some general disorder. One noontime, the usual kettle of brown, watery soup was left outside on a table. Normally, the one in charge would delegate somebody to ladle the soup and organize the rest of us to line up. But now there was nobody to do this. Mother stepped into the role and started bringing the soup in to people. Then suddenly we heard a loud boom and crash. The ground quaked. The first bomb. Then another bomb. Then a full bombardment was underway.

Russian airplanes were circling the camp. One bomb exploded nearby, hitting our ward and blasting shrapnel into our barracks. Some women were hit and bleeding from the wounds. Quite a few were injured badly. But the bombs and mayhem didn't keep Mother from her mission. She continued to go out with a few bowls, fill them up with the thickest part of the soup from the bottom of the kettle, bring them back in to us and dole it out in portions. When she finished, she started to attend to the wounded.

The planes flew past and it was quiet for a few minutes before we heard another group. Mother said this was a good sign. "We will be alright. We will survive," she told everybody. "Be brave. Don't lose hope or courage. It is coming to an end."

Some women looked at Mother and said, "Are you crazy? Don't you see? It's coming to an end, but it's our end."

Other people were happy to hear the bombardment. Even if we died, so too would our torturers. Despite everything, Mother kept on track. She insisted that the war would be over soon and we would be free. She didn't let the negativity of the others affect her. She didn't stop portioning out the soup or tending to the wounded.

The bombing went on for some weeks. It was around the beginning of spring, 1945. There were also mortar attacks from the ground.

Portions of the camp were burning. Outside, we heard the rumbling of trucks and the loudspeaker blaring. Everyone able to walk was to come out of the barracks. "Save yourself," it said.

We went outside and stood in groups, waiting. It took them a few minutes but the remaining SS finally came and lined us up in rows. They told us that the Russians were not too far away and that we were going to be taken to a boat. They told us that if we remained, the Russians would kill us. They made it seem like we had a choice, but we didn't have a choice. We were marched out of the camp. It was emptied of all except those in the hospital who were too sick and unable to walk.

My legs were feeble and atrophied. I could hardly stand anymore but now I had to walk. We started in the late afternoon. It was spring. The air was cool and the fields around us were wet and turning green. All of us were on the verge of collapse. We walked holding and supporting each other for miles. On one side of us, the SS troops marched. There was one soldier about every few meters. If somebody should fall or fall behind, they were instantly shot. I remember the echoing crack of the rifle when it first went off near the back of the rows of people. I never looked back but soon a pistol shot went off ahead of us too. We would occasionally have to step over a body. Where one of us had fallen and been shot or simply dropped back in line from fatigue, the gap in the rows would close quickly and we would try not to let the guards notice.

They eyed us constantly, ready to pull their pistols and squash us like insects with their bullets. I could tell that the Germans were at the end of their rope, losing the war. Some of the guards were outwardly frustrated and they wanted us dead so that we couldn't speak about their crimes. Other guards didn't care and seemed to look like they didn't want to be there. We marched for hours into the night without stopping. Surprisingly, an officer threw a piece of bread at me. I hadn't had bread for a long time and the hunger clouded my thinking so I picked it up. It could have been a trap. One of the officers nearby to the other officer said, "What are you doing?"

The officer who threw the bread replied, "In a few days, the war will be over. It doesn't make a difference anymore."

The officer didn't shoot me. The incident passed. I gave some of the bread to Mother and Etka and ate the rest myself. Even with the bread my body had grown too weak to continue walking on my own. Mother and Etka took turns linking their arms with mine until we reached the boats moored at Hela Harbor. At the harbor, there were many prisoners from neighboring camps as well as those of us from Stutthof, mainly women at that point, waiting to board two barges. One boat was just for the sick, the other was for the rest of us.

Once we were loaded onto the boat, it set out upon the cold, gray sea. We didn't know where we were being taken or why. We just knew that things were going badly for Germany. This made us more afraid. I thought to myself, "They are going to drown us now. After all that we went through, we will drown." But as long as the guards were with us, we knew they wouldn't sink the boat. That didn't mean they wouldn't shoot us or do something else. The boat sailed in circles for over a week. We had no food or water. Somehow, somebody managed to retrieve some salt water and we drank it. It didn't slake our thirst though. Overhead, we could see the Allied planes flying past on their way to or from some mission.

The Germans never stated our destination and I don't think they themselves knew what to do. The boat docked in a few harbors where it picked up some more people. Other times it would start to dock and get turned away. We bounced from harbor to harbor aimlessly. We figured that it was only a matter of time before they did away with us. We knew that in the end their intention was to drown us, to bury their crime beneath the waves of the Baltic. But why would they wait so long?

We finally anchored in shallow water not too far from some shoreline. A rumor started to spread that the SS had abandoned the boat and left us there on our own to be bombed by the Allied planes or to drown or drift until we died. As usual, Mother had to find out what was going on. She immediately went around the boat to investigate. She saw no Germans anywhere on the ship and decided we had to leave.

We could see the shore from where we were. It was within swimming distance. Mother and a few others found some boards and tossed them in the water to be used as floats because we didn't know how to swim. People began to jump into the ocean and grab onto the boards. Mother told me I had to go with her first and that she would come back for Etka. She jumped into the water and called me down after her. I didn't think twice and jumped. The water was shockingly cold. I floundered and reached for the board. I grabbed it and held tightly. Mother then grabbed my arm and turned us toward shore. She began kicking.

When we arrived, Mother walked me out of the water and across a small strip of shoreline rocks to a low bluff covered with grass. She sat me down and told me to wait. She waded back into the water and grabbed our floating board. She returned about a half an hour later with Etka. We didn't know what to do or where to go and just sat down on the grass to wait. Many other people did exactly as we did. There were a few hundred of us sitting on that grass looking out over the Baltic's Lubeck Bay. Others remained on the boat and waited to be rescued. We continued to watch as the Allied planes buzzed past overhead and flew out to sea.

Looking out at our boat, I could see that the SS had returned and those who had remained on the boat were being shot and dumped overboard, or pushed and kicked into the sea and then shot as they fell into the frigid water. Their unbearable screams were soon silenced as they slipped under the waves. It was a terrible scene to witness. The hope we held just a few minutes earlier while waiting on that strip of grass turned quickly once more to terror as the SS appeared on shore. They ordered us to line up in an orderly fashion. They said that they were going to transfer us to a different ship but that we were going to get some food before boarding.

These were the Nazi's last days and still they wanted to pursue us, to hunt and haunt us. They began walking us in our lines to the place where we would embark. They ordered that whoever refused to follow or whoever couldn't walk straight would be shot. My legs were weak. They hardly had any flesh or any muscle on them. I couldn't walk any further and started to fall behind. I slowed until I was at the back of the line. Mother had fallen back with me, supporting me as much as she could. An SS officer noticed me stumbling and rushed over with his hand on the trigger of his carbine, ready to aim and pull it. Mother leaned down and commanded in a stern whisper, "You can walk and you will!"

The SS men yelled, "Hey, you Jüde!"

Mother grabbed my arm firmly and yanked upward. "You don't want to be killed in front of me do you?" she declared.

I straightened up and started marching with my last ounce of energy. My legs felt wobbly but I made it to the departure point. We were in a place called Neustadt Holstein. We were told to wait to be loaded onto a small boat. From there, we were going to be taken out to sea and loaded onto a larger ship called the *Cap Arcona*. They commanded us to follow them to a building where we would get some food. But I couldn't walk anymore and collapsed. Mother saw this, looked around and said, "Just stay here, nobody will notice." She said she would be right back with something to eat for me. I was sitting there alone, trying to remain upright when an SS man noticed me. He asked why I wasn't with the others, pointed his pistol, and ordered me to get up. I put my hand on the ground and slowly pushed myself to my feet.

By the time I reached a full standing position and looked up, the SS man was gone. He had vanished. I was relieved but scared. Then, out of nowhere, another man appeared. He had a youthful sense about him with a pleasant face that was very light in appearance. He wore white clothes and was so tall he had to bend down far to see me. On his hip, he had a little bag of flour and he gestured to see if I wanted some. I was hesitant but nodded, "Yes." He motioned that I should stretch my hand out, palm up. I did as instructed and he filled my palm with white flour. I licked it. Then he was gone. He appeared one moment and was gone in another moment. It was a surreal happening but a very real experience. These were the last moments of the war and my body was near shutting down. Starving, with little physical strength or mental focus, I could not say to where the SS man had disappeared or from where the man in white had appeared. I am only grateful that it happened.

Soon Mother and Etka returned. They were rushing toward me and had joy and excitement on their faces. In their hands they held chocolate, cookies and gum. The British had tossed the sweets from their tanks as they passed they told me. I couldn't believe my eyes. I hadn't seen this kind of happiness in such a long time. We were free. It was unbelievable, overwhelming. For so long, we had waited for this moment. It was like a dream. It couldn't possibly be coming true. But it was true. It had come true. The nightmare was ended. The war was over. To this day, I do not know who the man in white with the flour was, but he gave me my first taste of liberation. It was May 3, 1945. On this date every year since, I have poured some raw flour into my palm and licked it exactly as I did then, thinking of the joy of our liberation, the miracle of our survival.

But there would be one last tragedy on that afternoon of liberation, one last horror that turned the ocean's waves red with blood. As Mother and Etka returned with the gifts from the British soldiers, a bombardment by British planes began out at sea. The planes roared across the sky and their bombs exploded onto the ships docked in the shallow water below. Rockets and machine gun fire followed, but they were firing on ships filled with thousands of Jewish concentration camp prisoners. One of the ships, the *Cap Arcona*, a giant ocean liner, was the ship we were supposed to have boarded.

The waves of bombings decimated the vessels. I sat on shore and watched. I couldn't understand why the planes were bombing. I watched people, Jewish prisoners, leaping from the high decks into the sea. I watched the planes fly past, strafing. I watched as the bombs exploded and filled the sky with evaporating plumes of steel gray smoke. I watched the furious red flames burn the ships and the people on them. I watched as the sea grew bloody and the waves lifted dead bodies gently up and down. I watched the whole scene played out in just fifteen or twenty minutes. Then it was over and I watched the hulking mass of the *Cap Arcona* capsize and sink slowly beneath the icy waves.

Nearly everyone on board the ships died. Only a few hundred survived or were rescued. During the next several days, thousands of corpses washed up on shore, the Baltic giving up its dead. They were collected and buried in a mass grave where, later, a memorial was dedicated. Being there on that shoreline was the first time I had ever seen the ocean, the first time I really had a chance to sit and look at it. It was not an ocean of beauty; it was an ocean of tragedy. I had come to this ocean of tragedy by way of a place called Neustadt Holstein. I had come to Neustadt Holstein by way of the Stutthof concentration camp. Before that I had come by way of Auschwitz and the Łódź ghetto. Prior to all this, I had known a good life in a city called Łódź. It was my home, and was filled with light, warmth and love. Then life became a stranger to me, gray, cold and distant. Life took me on a journey of unimaginable things. From one minute to the next, nothing was certain; misery, fear, and devastation were everywhere.

Chapter 13

The day of our liberation was the start of another great journey. Before any of us could find a way to move forward with our lives, we had to help our bodies become healthy. Years of malnutrition had built up and continued to ravage people even after liberation. Scores of survivors were hospitalized because they were sick, weak, and unable to digest any food. Disease was still present, people's bodies were still weak and sick, and most of us didn't know where to go or what to do. But at least we didn't have to suffer the same starvation diet of watery soup and stale bread, the same daily torture and anxiety.

One of the tragic after-effects of those years was that food became poison. Doctors were issuing orders and word spread that we should eat only small amounts of certain foods so that our systems could readjust to normal nutrition. But many people didn't listen and died. For others, help arrived too late. Their bodies were too decimated by the constant, extreme hunger and nothing could be done to revive them.

British doctors at a former German Navy hospital in Neustadt Holstein examined Mother, Etka and me. Our bodies were just skeletons but we were checked out as okay and didn't have to stay which was good because the hospital beds were all being used by those who desperately needed them. Mother took special care to make sure we didn't overdo it with the food we were given. We were the only people that remained of our family as far as we knew, and she would not have us die after coming this far. She demanded that we eat only in moderation until our stomachs got used to food. Getting healthy would be our biggest concern for those first few months. Later we would face the bitter truth and difficult task of searching out the survivors and the deceased among our family and friends. In the back of our minds, we hoped to find them all still alive. But we knew that this was unlikely.

Mother, Etka and I had no desire to go back to Poland. We had

107

heard stories of people returning only to find that the anti-Semitism had gotten worse, only to find that instead of Germans brutalizing Jews, the Polish people were the perpetrators. What was there to go back to anyway? Our homes, our families, our communities were gone. What we treasured and loved was destroyed. We were displaced people, refugees. Other countries hadn't yet opened their borders to us for immigration and going back to where we came from wasn't an option.

The United Nations Relief and Rehabilitation Administration (UNNRA) was the first administrative agency to provide refugee assistance. UNRRA registered us and distributed food and clothing. Later, the American Jewish Joint Distribution Committee was also central in helping with clothing and food distribution, and with creating a list of survivors. Neustadt Holstein was in the British Zone. In every zone, UNRRA had set up *Displaced Persons* camps. In Neustadt, the agency set aside an area of abandoned buildings, mostly German Navy quarters, for us to live in. The D.P. camp in Neustadt housed survivors from all over Europe: Poland, Romania, Czechoslovakia, Hungary, Germany, France, Lithuania, and Russia. Everywhere I went I heard different languages spoken. Yiddish became the common language. Most of us knew and could understand enough to make it a valuable way to communicate.

Within the camp, everybody settled where he or she could find space. As we were walking into the area that UNRRA set aside for us, Mother noticed an empty barrack. We went inside. The place was huge. The ceilings were high and there was a vast hall with long, narrow windows that extended from floor to ceiling. Later, our friends would jokingly use the windows as doors. There were many beds where we could rest our exhausted bodies. There was also a kitchen with a stove and a refrigerated cooler. We considered ourselves lucky. For the next few years, this would be our home.

We searched around the building and discovered boxes filled with blankets and some containing blue outfits and underwear–Navy uniforms. We found some other clothing on the floor, simply scattered as if it was dropped there in haste. The attacks likely caught the Germans off guard and sent them running to hide, or else, as many did, they just changed into civilian clothes and walked away, mixing in with the local population of fishermen, escaping unrecognized. No one was looking for them at the time. In fact, shortly after we settled into the building a few Germans in civilian clothing came in and, without saying anything, went upstairs to the second floor. I didn't know what they were doing but they retrieved some documents and left.

Happy to have blankets and beds, and being very tired, we laid down to sleep. Mother was restless and unable to sleep and woke up after about an hour. She knew that there was still much to be done. Determined to get us some food and despite the painful sores and aches of her feet, she went outside to search for food and other supplies. She and some other survivors noticed a warehouse in the area. The doors were closed and locked, but a couple of people scavenged some tools and broke the latch on the doors. Inside, they discovered a food warehouse. It was mostly empty, but in one section a few hundred-pound bags of salt and sugar remained. Somebody sliced open a bag of sugar and it streamed out all over the floor. They took tastes of it but had no way to scoop it up to take it home. Most of the group went on to look someplace else. "What could we do with a hundred pound bag of salt or sugar?" they thought.

That's exactly what Mother thought as well. Plus, she was too tired to go look for food someplace else. She found a wagon outside and brought it in to load one of the bags of salt. But it was too heavy and she couldn't lift it. She asked two of the remaining men from the group to help her. Thin, starving, and feeble looking, the men responded, "Lady, what do you need a hundred pounds of salt for?"

Mother answered, "If you help me to take it home, I have all kinds of pants, jackets, underwear, and blankets that the soldiers left behind. When we get there, I will share them with you. I am sure you need and could use them."

They consented and lifted the bag of salt onto the wagon along with a hundred pound bag of sugar that they wanted for themselves. It wasn't too far to pull the wagon back to our place. We were excited to see them and wanted to know what was in the sacks. "Salt for us and sugar for the men," mother told us.

The men decided to leave the sugar at our place. Mother went into the kitchen and came back with a knife. She handed it to one of the men, then went into the kitchen again and returned with a few big pots. One of the men sliced into the bag of sugar and let it pour out into his pot. Then they filled up another. Mother gave them blankets, jackets and underwear and thanked them.

"If you are ever in need of salt, please come back. You can have as much as you need," she told them. They nodded and left. By now, Mother was out of breath. We told her that we should all get some rest and wake up refreshed. She agreed. We licked a bit of the sugar, its sweetness still strange to me, and fell asleep.

The next morning Etka and I asked Mother why she had chosen salt over sugar and why we would need one hundred pounds of salt. "Now that we are liberated, my children," she said, "we can start cooking. And salt is more important than sugar. You cannot do without it. I will give the salt away to people who need it and it exchange it for other things we may need." She was right. Nobody had salt, so people came to us to get it. We gave away the extra uniforms, underwear, and blankets to anybody who needed or wanted them.

Through UNRRA we received cans of ham, sausages, sardines, fruit, coffee, cocoa, tea, cigarettes, and clothing. As time went on, a Jewish committee was established by electing some of the refugee men. This made administration in the camp much easier. We registered again with this Jewish council. They helped with food and clothing distribution and became the center of information on who was still alive. We used the UNRRA food sparingly in the beginning to avoid poisoning our delicate and sensitive digestive systems. Once our stomachs expanded and we got used to meat and the other foods we hadn't had in years, we were able to eat normally. Bread, together with the soup that had been the staple of our diet for the past five years, was in short supply.

One morning after her health had improved, Mother went downtown to search out a bakery. Even though it was against regulations, she brought UNRRA coffee and cigarettes with her to trade in case she found one. The Germans loved coffee but had no way of obtaining it on their own. Mother had heard of other people selling or trading UNRRA products on the black-market and even though she didn't want to violate the rules, she was determined to get some much needed bread or some flour to bake our own bread.

Mother found a bakery and went inside. The baker was wary of the exchange, concerned that if he was caught with the coffee and cigarettes, he could be arrested. Mother assured him that he would be safe, that nobody would know and that she wouldn't tell. Besides, it was an honest transaction to help a Jewish family and helping is what the coffee and cigarettes had been intended to do. Still, the baker was hesitant and instead simply gave Mother some bread and flour, refusing the trade.

She went back a second time and the baker accepted the goods in trade. Mother's visits became regular and he even started to look forward to them. Once, I went on the errand instead of Mother. The baker was sorry Mother couldn't come but said that it was pleasant to meet the "good woman's" daughter. It was still strange to have relatively normal interaction with a German. I had no idea if this man had been a Nazi, if he had sympathized, if he had hated the Nazi's, or if he had just been a baker in a seaside town. It didn't really cross my mind at the time. I was still surviving and the goal was to get bread. The baker gave me some bread and rolls. He said he had put them aside as usual for Mother and wished me a safe trip back.

It turns out that everybody was trading cigarettes and coffee. Some of the refugees bought bikes and would ride down to a nearby farm to pick up chickens, eggs, and cheese in trade. They brought the food back and sold it where they could. If they couldn't sell, they would trade. Frequently they came to our place to trade for salt or sugar. Because of Mother's ingenuity, we had a variety of ingredients to make meals and gradually regained our strength and health.

As our bodies healed, a new fever developed. That fever was the urge to find information on family members. We filled out paperwork and handed it in to UNRRA and the Jewish Joint Distribution Committee to be listed as survivors, hoping that somewhere else other members of our family were doing the same. But this was not enough and many people traveled between the D.P. camps seeking out their loved ones, someone who knew their loved ones, or people they had known before the war.

Many people traveled to Neustadt Holstein to find information. In 1945, the British erected a cemetery in the town for the thousands of Jews who were gunned down by Germans when their legs and feet gave out on the long march to the sea, who lost their lives to the bombings of the ships at sea, who died from starvation, or whose stomachs exploded at the first experience of real nutrition. In 1946, headstones were put on the graves at the cemetery in compliance with Jewish tradition. Some of the buried were unknown, others known only by a number. Still, survivors would come from all over to seek out their family member's names on the headstones. If they didn't find what they were looking for, they were both happy and sad. It might mean that the person being sought was still alive. If they found the name of someone they were looking for, they cried and prayed, asked for blessings and for God to have mercy on the soul of the departed.

Mother had heard from somebody that many survivors from Poland were living in the D.P. camp in Bergen-Belsen. It was about two hours drive away from us. She found a ride with somebody and went searching for news of our family. When she arrived, she met somebody who had been in a concentration camp with Moshe Bogen, Aunt Mania's old flame. The person told mother that Moshe had survived and was living there in Bergen-Belsen. She sought him out to see if he knew anything about Aunt Mania. When she found him, the reunion was bittersweet. Although they were happy to see each other, Moshe did not know what happened to Aunt Mania. He did, however, give Mother something precious to keep. He unexpectedly handed her two photographs that had been taken before the war. One was a photo of Aunt Mania. The other was a group photo of our family and some friends taken one summer on the outskirts of Helenowek.

He told Mother that, after the liberation, he was one of the few who returned to Poland to search for his family and the remnants of his former life. He didn't find anyone alive, but did go back to where he and his family had lived in the Łódź ghetto to recover some photos he had hidden. As luck would have it, the photos were still there. The two pictures he gave Mother were among them.

Mother parted with Moshe, leaving our address with him and imploring him to stay in touch. When she returned, she showed Etka and me the photographs. I was filled briefly with the happiness of those summers when Moshe would accompany Aunt Mania to the countryside to see us. I looked at the smiling faces but then couldn't look anymore.

Eventually, we came to learn that everybody in our family was killed. Mother, Etka, and I were the only survivors. It was a miracle that we survived together. We never knew how they died, but we found out that our beloved brother, Icek and Father had been killed. We learned the story of what happened to Father when Etka, on her way to her new home in South America via Paris, met an old neighbor from Łódź who had been part of the party who escaped to Baranowicz with Father. She told Etka as much as she knew about what happened to him, saying that when it became apparent that the Germans were attacking, people began fleeing further east. Father stayed because he wanted to wait for us. That was all our old neighbor knew. We searched archives and records and found no trace of him. Most likely, he died when the Jewish people in Baranowicz were sent to concentration camps after the Germans took the city.

Father's sister, Aunt Fradla, her husband, Uncle Heskel and their family were also dead as was Aunt Mania, her husband and new baby. Aunt Sarah had been killed. Feigi Leah also. Uncle Mayer's daughters, Chana and Ethel. And Father's only brother, Asher, gone too. Everybody in our family except the three of us was gone. One mother and two daughters, were all that was left of so much warmth, so much hope, so much love.

Chapter 14

"Neustadt" means "New Town" in German. In this new town, I started a new life with new hopes and new fears. We were liberated, but not free. It was still Germany, we were still refugees, and, in a sense, still closed in. We didn't know where we would ultimately go or if we would all be together. We did our best to make things normal and livable, but were also eager to find a permanent place to settle, to find a community, security, routine, and to live a normal existence.

Life in Neustadt Holstein and the DP camp was a life in transition. With no work, there was no schedule. We spent our days searching for information on family, waiting out the very slow process of getting immigration approval, meeting new people and making friends, drinking soda and dancing at the canteen, and creating a semblance of home. There was a lot of mourning and a lot of healing in the D.P. camp, but also some moments of joy. We were filled with a great desire to start fresh, to mend our lives and begin anew. For some reason or another, everybody wanted to connect with somebody. Getting married was one of the ways people connected. Weddings were very special occasions and there were many of them. People took great delight in them. They symbolized renewal and continuation of life.

In 1946, like many, I got married to a young Polish survivor who also lived in the D.P. camp. We didn't know each other previously, but he too was from Łódź. Everybody in the camp was invited to the ceremony because everybody was like family. The whole community pitched in to make a traditional Jewish wedding for us, and UNRRA provided food for the subsequent banquet. Before the ceremony, I had to travel by car to the closest *mikvah* in Bergen-Belsen. I didn't travel in those days and hadn't been in a car in a long time, so the trip made me terribly nauseous. The car took so long getting back to Neustadt

Holstein that people began to wonder if something had happened. But we finally made it and the ceremony took place.

I wore a white dress and a veil that I borrowed from another woman. I walked in that dress from our home with the tall windows to the little *shtuebel* that had been made as a place for people to pray. There, we got our *ketubah*, our marriage certificate, and held the ceremony outside, under the open sky. A Torah was brought in and there was a very plain, linen chuppa. Afterward, everybody went to our place where a long banquet table was set up. Our tall windows became the doors that welcomed people in to laugh, eat, and celebrate.

My husband was twenty and I was nineteen. We were both struggling to catch up to our years, to heal, and to move forward. But we were young and naïve and didn't know much about marriage. While it was difficult and wouldn't last, it was well worth it. On April 2, 1947, I got a wonderful gift. That day I gave birth to my first child, a beautiful baby boy named Chuck. He became my treasure, my life and my joy.

Etka was also married in 1946 to a man named Shlomo, another survivor. Shlomo ran a canteen in Bergen-Belsen. They had worked in the same place in the ghetto and known each other. Shlomo traveled to Neustadt Holstein to make some purchases and spotted Etka on the street. She recognized him, too. Shlomo then invited Etka to Bergen-Belsen, showered her with little gifts, and doted upon her. Shortly after, with Mother's blessing, Shlomo and Etka got married. Their ceremony was a very exciting moment and gave everybody in the camp something special to look forward to and to talk about.

Our new families wanted badly to leave Germany and start out lives. Israel, America, Canada or Sweden was a top destination. So we all registered with the Jewish Agency and waited, hoping to get passage to one of these places. It took some time, but countries gradually started to open their doors to us. Sweden was one of the first to open up, but was only taking those survivors who had specific professions, skills or trades. Many Jewish professionals jumped at the chance and went to Sweden. Canada was next in opening its doors to refugees. Many people left for Canada and a new life there.

A few months after I had Chuck, Etka and Shlomo had their first son, Schmuel. He was born on November 18, 1947. With the birth of their son, they wanted more than anything to leave Germany. Shlomo had a brother who had moved to Argentina many years before the war. Shlomo's brother found out that Shlomo was alive and had written Shlomo an ecstatic letter. Shlomo responded with his own letter. In it, he wrote that two of their other brothers had survived as well. They had all found new brides. Shlomo's brother was so happy to hear the good news. He promised to try to the utmost of his ability to get his brothers out of Germany, to be reunited with family and make a better life in Argentina.

Unfortunately, at the time, it was impossible for Jewish refugees to obtain a visa even if you had close relatives in a country. Shlomo inquired with the Jewish Agency as to what he should do. They told him to go to France for a year to establish residency because it would be easier to obtain a visa from France. The Jewish Agency would help them when the year had passed. As advised, Etka and Shlomo decided to leave for France as soon as they could. Mother didn't want them to go. I, too, wanted them to wait. I thought that if we waited a little longer, we could all gain entry to America and be together. But we understood their desire to leave to find a better life. We also wanted badly to get out of Germany. Being there was like purgatory. We couldn't go this way and we couldn't go that way.

The day they left was emotional and filled with many hugs and kisses. I was sad but hopeful for their journey. Mother blessed them and wished them safe travels. We bade them good luck and told them that when next we see each other we wanted to see them doing well. Etka said she would write, and then we said tearful goodbyes and promised to see each other again as soon as it became possible.

Etka, Shlomo, their baby Schmuel and Shlomo's two brothers with their families traveled to France, found rooms and settled there. They had to find jobs because a job was required to establish residency. From there, they could apply for visas to any country neighboring Argentina. Then, the Jewish Agency would do what it could to help them get across the Argentine border, but mostly they would be on their own in getting to their final destination.

A year passed and the Jewish Agency helped them ready visas for Paraguay. The plan was to stop in Uruguay on their way to the inland country and instead catch a boat to Argentina. They carried out their plan without a hitch as far as Uruguay. But in trying to take the boat to Argentina, they were stopped and the men arrested. The Jewish Agency worked tirelessly to get them released and succeeded. Once released, they made their way to Argentina and reunited with Shlomo's brother. Etka wrote us and told us the whole story. I was overjoyed that they had arrived safely.

Through the years we kept in touch, first by letter, then by phone. Etka wrote us often that Shlomo and she were disappointed and often sorry that they had settled in Argentina. She regretted that they hadn't waited for us so that we would all have ended up in the same place together. The climate also didn't agree with them and their path toward making a decent living was filled with hardships. We received a letter from Etka shortly after we had made it to the US. She said that she wanted so much to be with us and asked if it was possible for us to help them get visas. Of course we would help them. We were happy that they wanted to leave Argentina. Twice we did all the necessary paperwork and twice they changed their minds.

Things eventually got better for them. They worked day and night to establish their business—a small textile factory. It began to do well and they had another son named Isaac. Once Isaac was born, they let go of their dream to move to the United States. Widowed now, Etka resides in Buenos Aires. Her son Shmuel married Silvia and had two children, Gustavo and Judith. Her second son, Isaac, married Monica and also had two children, Izakiel and Lucila.

Back in Neustadt Holstein, Mother and I registered to go to the United States. It was a highly desired destination and there was a long wait for approval. The first people allowed entrance to the States were those who had relatives who would sponsor them. Others with special status were also given special consideration. We had no relatives in the U.S. and no cause for special consideration, so we waited two years. But the Jewish Agency was instrumental in helping us with the immigration process and, in 1949, they gave us wonderful news: we had been accepted. Pending a successful physical checkup and after a thorough examination of our papers to see that they were in the proper order, we would be able to travel to the United States.

Our bodies by then were well recovered and, as Mother had said would happen, my hair grew backer thicker and fuller than before, but the examination made us anxious. Many people were rejected because they had some temporary illness that happened to strike at just the wrong time. Also, we'd heard that the review of the papers would turn up anything even slightly imperfect. If we failed the physical or our papers weren't in perfect order, we would be moved to the back of the line and have to wait perhaps years again. We also didn't know if we would be approved together or if we would have to separate.

Luckily, to our extreme delight, our papers were in order and we passed the physicals. The only disappointment was that Mother would have to come on a later voyage. It was scheduled for only two weeks later but it was another source of anxiety. The moment we had been waiting for had finally arrived. Our time in Neustadt, a time of waiting, a time of continuing to struggle to overcome, a time where I learned to treasure life under all circumstance, good and bad, was finally ending.

On October 9, 1949, we boarded a ship bound for America. The ship was called the *USS General Mauer*. It was an old, second-class ship. Our lodgings were adequate and we were excited to be going to the land of our dreams. Chuck was about two and a half at the time. He contracted chicken pox during the voyage. The ship's doctor told us that he had to be quarantined. I felt terrible for him and wanted so much to be able to take care of him, but I had no choice. I was allowed to watch him from a distance and was also able to speak to him. He and the other children in quarantine received great care from the nurses and doctors. They gave the children toys and medication, and after a few days, he was discharged and I could hold him in my arms for the remainder of our voyage.

Crossing the Atlantic Ocean was long and tiring. The final stretch was especially turbulent and storm-tossed. When we arrived in New York I was exhausted and perpetually seasick. We registered and showed our papers. Then a representative of the Jewish Agency came over with a list in his hands. He took us to get some food and asked if there was particular city or town that we desired as our final destination. We had no relatives and knew little about the country so one place was as good as another. The representative asked if it would be okay if we were sent to Rochester, New York.

"Of course," we told him.

We went to Rochester by airplane. I had never been on a plane and was very excited for the trip. Arriving in Rochester, we were met at the airport by a Jewish Family Service member, a man by the name of Boyer. Because our young marriage had been problematic, my husband and I decided at this point to go our separate ways. Later, we would be officially divorced. Boyer took Chuck and me to get some food and then brought us to a home owned by an elderly woman and her husband. The elderly woman and her husband gave us one bedroom upstairs and the use of their kitchen. The Jewish Family Service paid the rent and helped us with a stipend to be used for groceries and other living expenses. Mother arrived in Rochester from Neustadt Holstein a few weeks later and we found a new apartment with more space.

Adjusting to life in Rochester took time. Life was still filled with challenges and lessons that I could only learn with experience. Nevertheless, there was no danger of being shot or killed for no reason at all, no threat of a malicious beating, no sudden uprooting, no rampant starvation, no typhus epidemic, dysentery or diarrhea, and no program of dehumanization. It felt good to be free and unafraid. It felt even better to have our dignity and a sense of opportunity.

Despite everything being foreign and new, it wasn't long before we settled into a regular life. A friend found me a job, Chuck was enrolled in preschool, and I began taking night classes in English. I had had some instruction before I left Germany, but it wasn't the same as being immersed in the language. Besides the night classes, I learned from listening to people, speaking with my coworkers, watching television, and reading. I approached English like it was my own language, like it was the language I was born with. I loved the new language and tried never to speak Polish, though I still had to use Polish to correspond with my sister who now was learning to speak Spanish in her new home of Argentina.

In time, I became a U.S. citizen and my name was changed from Marysia to Marian. Prior to going before the judge to change my name, a friend urged, "You have to have an American name." I didn't know what name. I like the sound of Marian so when I went before the judge and he asked me what I wanted my name to be, I said, "Marian." The judge asked, "How do you want it spelled, with an 'a' or an 'o?' " I didn't really know, so I said, "An 'a.'"

I lived in Rochester from 1949 to 1955 when I married Isak Kampinski and moved to Cleveland, Ohio. Isak was from a small town in Poland called Lutitov. He was also a survivor who had been in many concentration and work camps. He did forced labor in coalmines and building railroads, and had lost all but one brother in a family of ten children. After the war, we were in the D.P. camp in Neustadt Holstein together. We didn't know each other well, but Mother had strong ties to him and had kept in touch after we moved to the US. He was sent to Cleveland when he arrived in America.

Mother had some friends who had moved to Columbus, Ohio, who visited us often in Rochester. They were responsible for bringing Isak and me together. They happened to be visiting us once at the same time I was about to take a vacation from work. I wanted to go to the mountains to get away from the city but Mother's friends convinced me to go back to Columbus with them. They said we could go to Cleveland and visit some mutual friends from the D.P. camp. I went and had a great time. Our friends threw a big party for me. Everybody we knew came. Isak came, too. He wanted to see me and asked to take me out, but I was hesitant. I went back to Rochester and back to work. Isak didn't give up. He started to write and came to visit a few times. Our correspondence continued and I grew fond of him. Finally, he came to Rochester and asked me to marry him but I wasn't ready to answer. I thought seriously about his proposal. I thought about Chuck, about Mother, and about leaving Rochester. Mother counseled that Isak was a good man who would be a good husband and father. When I gave him the answer, it was yes.

We married in 1956 and moved to Cleveland. Isak worked and I was a stay-at-home mom. I gave birth to my second child, Nancy in 1958, then to Anita in 1960, and Jack in 1961. My children were my full time job. They gave me the happiest years of my life. Seeing them develop, go to school, find their freedom, and achieve their goals was my greatest joy. Each one was a like a new flower that had to be watered, nurtured, and guided. It was beautiful to watch them grow. I was always there and we were very close no matter how difficult. I wanted to keep them safe and unafraid, to make their home a sanctuary. I wanted them to be able to say, "My parents are here" in a way that I could not say. It gave me so much pleasure to work with them when they had trouble with schoolwork, to go to PTA meetings, to take them to piano lessons or art lessons, or to take them shopping.

My children were the new beginning that made everything worthwhile. They made every day a beautiful, lasting experience, becoming the new generation, the next branches of our family tree. They are the proof that Hitler and the Nazis had not succeeded in their insidious "Final Solution." They had not destroyed our spirit or our hearts. They had only destroyed themselves.

Mother lived in Cleveland also, but always maintained a passion for Israel. Her love of Israel was deep in her heart. In 1960, she received some compensation money from the German government and traveled to Israel for the first time. While there, she visited with all kinds of people she knew. Her visit only deepened her love for Israel. She wanted to relocate there but would only think of moving if we all would. When Mother got older she began to spend winters in Florida because she couldn't deal with the Cleveland cold. In Florida, she met a Cantor named Abe Hoffman. They developed a friendship and affection that blossomed into a happy marriage. Together, they decided to move to Israel where most of Abe's family had moved after the war. They packed two suitcases each and left. Mother was sixty years old when she achieved her dream of living in Israel.

Later in life, Mother developed abdominal cancer. She was living in Netanya with Abe. My daughter Nancy had finished college in Israel and settled there, where she married and started her own family. Nancy was working as a registered nurse in a hospital and living in a town not too far away from Mother. I remained in Cleveland with Isak. My son, Chuck, was also living in Cleveland with his family and working as a successful lawyer. My youngest son, Jack, lived in Cleveland, too. My other daughter Anita, like her sister, studied in Israel and, after getting her degree, decided to stay to become a teacher. Etka and Shlomo were in Argentina with their children.

Mother and I traveled to visit each other when we could, but it was difficult. When I found out about the cancer, I made plans to travel from Cleveland to Israel the next Sunday. But the doctor advised that Mother would have to undergo surgery right away. Mother told the doctor it would have to wait until I arrived. Unable to convince Mother of the importance of doing this procedure now, the doctor asked Abe and Nancy for help. They both signed the necessary paperwork and Mother was brought into the operating room.

I arrived as planned on Sunday. By then, the procedure had already been completed. Nancy reassured me that everything had gone smoothly and that her *Bubbe* was fine. Then Nancy told me something astonishing. She had been waiting in the hall as Mother was wheeled from surgery to the recovery room and when the gurney passed, Mother, full of energy, exclaimed, "Hi Nancy!" and raised herself to a sitting position to talk. Nancy couldn't believe that her grandmother was so vibrant and lucid so soon after the operation.

"Bubbe, what happened? Didn't you just have your surgery?" she asked.

Mother replied, "You know I didn't have it done yet. I'm waiting for Marysia to come. When she comes, then I'll have the surgery."

Nancy was confused. Did Mother have the operation or not? If so, how could she be so quickly recovered? Nancy rushed to see the doctor. She asked him what had happened, told him that her grandmother just sat upright and said she didn't have the operation. The doctor looked just as confused and replied that she did have it. He had just finished it himself. He went in to check on Mother. She appeared fully recovered and already healed. "Thank God!" he said in disbelief. "We just witnessed a miracle."

From where Mother got her strength had always been a mystery to me. Through every trial, every obstacle, she was clear-headed, resolute, and hopeful. On the second afternoon after Mother had come home from the hospital, I was at her bedside and watched her fall asleep. I crept quietly out of her bedroom and closed the door, leaving it slightly ajar so that I could hear if something was wrong. Mother and I were the only people in the house. The nurse we had hired had not yet arrived for her shift and Abe was out getting groceries. There was a couch on a wall near a window where an air conditioner hummed silently and blew the thin curtains gently to the side. The couch looked inviting and I decided to lie down to rest. Soon my eyes were closed. The cool air drifted tenderly over me. I started to fall asleep when I sensed somebody moving in the house. I opened my eyes halfway and saw Mother slowly making her way, walker held tentatively out in front of her, toward me. Curious to see what she was up to, I kept my eyes half-closed and watched.

Carefully, holding tightly to her walker, she stepped closer to me. Through my cracked eyelids, I could see that there was a peaceful look on her face. She looked down at me briefly, then up at the air conditioner. Thinking that I was asleep, she took a blanket off of an adjacent chair and covered me with it up to the shoulders. Then she reached over to the air conditioner and lowered the speed of the fan. She turned and headed back to her room, moving carefully forward. Even when sick with cancer and ravaged by invasive surgery, Mother thought of her children first. She had come so far in life, been through so much hardship and pain, yet she was always our constant visible angel. She carried us through everything with wings held aloft by love and devotion. She transcended human strength in my eyes, giving me life in all its forms more than just in birth.

After her first surgery, it became clear that the cancer had progressed beyond maintenance or cure. Six months later, Mother fell deeply ill. She was in and out of the hospital frequently. One day, she called me from the hospital. She wanted to know how I was. She didn't complain one bit about her condition. She asked about my family and Chuck, then about Etka. She said that she had tried to phone Etka but that something was wrong with the phone lines and she couldn't reach her. I tried to call my sister but also could not get through. Finally, I looked up the number of a friend of my sister's and contacted that friend. The friend helped me reach Etka. When we spoke, I told her that Mother's condition was grave and that I could tell from Mother's voice that she wanted us to be there with her. I also lamented that I could not make the trip immediately because my husband was going into surgery himself. Without hesitation, Etka said that she and Shlomo would go. I promised to come as soon as I could.

Mother was in the hospital with Nancy when Etka and Shlomo arrived. Nancy had been at work when she experienced a sudden undeniable premonition. She left work immediately and rushed to see her grandmother. She arrived to find Mother in her last moments. She held her *Bubbe's* hand and said the *Shema Israel* with her. Etka and Shlomo had arrived with just enough time to speak briefly to Mother before she passed away. She died peacefully on May 15, 1984, some forty years after our liberation, in her beloved land of Israel. She was seventy-eight years old.

A year after Mother's death, just before the Shavuot holidays, I was able to travel to Israel from Cleveland to attend her stone setting. I was overcome with emotion and felt her presence everywhere. I knew that she would always be watching over us. On my visit, I stayed with Nancy who lived on the same street as a temple. We all walked to the temple for the holiday services to pray. Nancy, her daughter Shira, and I sat together. It came the time in the service to say the *Yiskor*, the prayers for the departed. All people whose parents were still alive left the temple and waited in the hallway until the prayers could be said. I was deep in prayer, saying *Yiskor* for Mother, Father, and others dearly departed when, to my astonishment, I opened my eyes to see a clear vision of Mother. She was standing in the front row of a line of benches perpendicular to the ones where I was sitting.

There was a woman next to her whom I instinctively thought was Mother's mother, the grandmother I had never met. The two women's faces looked strangely tranquil. Their heads were covered with a piece of white lace and each one had one arm where the skin looked like it was painted with a reddish, iodine-like substance. There was a depth to Mother's stare that took me aback. I knew that the two figures weren't real and tried to distract myself out of the illusion by looking away and continuing my prayers. But I couldn't look away. The apparitions were so real that I was mesmerized. I walked over a few steps and stopped a short distance from them. I tried to open my mouth to speak but couldn't. I was afraid. They looked very much alive and in the flesh, yet I knew they were not.

The time for prayers ended and I returned to my seat. When Nancy and Shira came back in, Nancy looked at me and said, "Mother what is wrong? You look like you have just seen a ghost."

"In fact, I did," I told her. Throughout my stay in Israel, I continued to have these visions, seeing Mother and the unknown woman everywhere. Somehow, I was comforted by their presence. Mother lives on in my thoughts forever. She is with me in heart and spirit. It was because of her determination, her selflessness, her will to live, and her love for her children that I am alive today.

Soon after Mother's stone setting, I returned to Cleveland where my husband and I have made a home for fifty-two years. Today, we escape Cleveland's frigid winters to the sunny and warm climes of Florida. Our apartment is right on the ocean; the beach is just outside our gate. I wake up daily at 5:00 a.m. to see the sun rising over the ocean. At 6:00 a.m., I walk along the boardwalk and look out at the water. It appears tranquil, untroubled, and serene. There is a smile on my face. Day by day, things come along and prove themselves reasons to rejoice. I walk quietly with my thoughts and memories. Some have grown more vague with time and some remain crystal clear. I know that we cannot recapture lost time, but maybe we can express the wisdom we have gained and seal it in the minds of the next generations. It seems evident that if we can teach the hearts of man to be kinder, better, and more peaceful then it will be a kinder, better, and more peaceful world.

There are still many unanswered questions and nightmarish memories from the Holocaust. Millions of Jews went to their deaths innocently, ashes blown into the wind, bones fallen into the earth, bodies drowned beneath the sea. But time helps to heal the wounds of those horrible years. Every morning I walk with a pen and a piece of paper in hand, recording my questions, my thoughts, and my poems. I feel at peace and I am happy to be free to pay attention to life's journey. I take refuge in my faith and live daily according to the last words my *Babcia* spoke to her children. "Be brave," she said. I also try to obey the instructions of the sallow looking man in the wheelchair from my dream as a child. "Never forget," he said. "Never forget."

I died more than six million deaths in the years of the Holocaust. I lost something or somebody every day. I lost neighbors, acquaintances, a country, a city, a home, a childhood, a father, brother, aunts, uncles, beloved cousins and friends, and more. I am all who were lost. I am David Getler, my father. I am Icek, my brother. I am Aunt Fradla and Uncle Heskel and their children, Aunt Mania and her tiny baby. I am Chana and Ethel. I am Hela and Hershel, Asher, and Feigi Leah. I am Mark and Ala and Roza. I am my neighbors and friends. I am all of them. Remember me.

Poems

Life's Treasure

My loving Mother
Life she was
Life she is
Life she loved
The gift of life
She treasured and lived

Faced with death
With the strength of a lion
Removed her challenge
Defeated all battles
She fought for life
And the pursuit worth living
Great faith in God believing

There was no time
For self pity
There was no time
To waste on tears
There was no time
For sadness or fears

Her only time
Was hers to love
To remove our worries
To comfort us
The force of strength
Whenever needed she was there

She took us children
Through drowning waters
And saved us
From burning fires
She guided us
And never tired

Her robes were life's
Pearls of wisdom
Faith, hope and courage
With a song and a smile
She danced to life
Her countless assets of values galore

Her children, grandchildren
And her great grandchildren
Loved and adored
She is our gift
Life's treasure
In our hearts alive forever
My loving Mother.

Who Am I?

I'm a person
I'm a life
I can breathe
Inhale the air
I have feelings
Capable of care
I'm a person

I feel sadness
I feel pain
I can laugh
And I can cry
I'm a person

I can see
I can look
I can read
Or write a book
I can hear
And I can talk
I can move
Or take a walk

I can smell
And I can taste
I can eat
And I can waste
I can think
And I can be
More and more

So much more
God gave to me
I'm free to choose
To be or not to be
Who am I?
I'm a person.

The Curse and The Blessing

Homeless, faceless, nameless
They call me beggar
I roam the streets
To find a corner
To throw my aching bones
Covered with beggar's rags
For a place to rest, to beg, to nest.

I fear the streets
Yet I drag my hurt, blistered feet
My shoes much too big
As I wander by day and night
I am a bundle of fright
The shadows approach my being
I pass many houses
Though none belong to me
I am a beggar.

The streets are gray
Cold and gloomy
As I cruise I shiver
From shame and pity
As warm and cold eyes
Mingle on the streets
Passing me by.

I sink and shrink
When a glance or a stare
With the tongue
Of a spear
And sting of a bee
Is aimed at me
As I walk the road of a beggar.

I am a beggar
Disabled with scars unseen
Men's handouts tossed at me
In silence without a word
Of a hello or good-bye
I feel belittled
In the hearts of man.

Am I less than a man
Or more than one
To carry the helpless
Daily course of hunger and pain
Stomach growling
Wounds unhealed
Freezing cold
And burning heat
Unleashed on my body
As I beg.

My hands outstretched
For others to fill
Disgrace and pity
I feel for myself
My throat is tickling dry
My eyes dripping wet
Watery, sorrowful tears
As the fall wet
To wash, to quiet my pain
The daily curse I bear

A helpless beggar am I
Despised by men for what I am
Yet I am your inner conscience
That reflects and opens your eyes to see
That poverty walks the streets
And I the beggar
Sometimes stare and melt

The hearts of steel
Into mercy and compassion.

This is my reward
To men for whether in rags or riches
There is a moral that teaches
That the image of God is lit before us
To bring forth concern for each other
As with one's brother
In me lies the curse and the blessing

Silently the World Stood By

Why oh why, I ask you why
Silently you stood by
When pain cried out
And echoed so loud.
When truth was known to you
You covered up its blackness
By silence and deafness
And went on pretending
As if not having a clue
As long as it wasn't
Happening to you.

Indifferent and immune
To the daily destruction
Aimed at the Jews
The hand of evil at work
Rage fused, atrocities, annihilations
Jewish roots eliminated
You stood by unmoved.
Why oh why, I ask of you why
Silently you stood by.

Break Your Silence

Our hearts are filled
With sorrow tears and pain
We carry – we carry
Our saintly remains

Intertwined in memories
Are horror lived visions
Choked by silence
Inability to speak
Inflicted by grief
In sorrow so thick
Stricken by inhuman severity
Nazi's evil – ran ocean deep

Break your silence
"Don't forget to tell"
Was death's plea
In a sigh of relief
Flowed your bitter tears
As your life ended
In up-torn years

With faintest hope
But promise calling
In search – to seek
To find – and not to despair
Maybe somewhere – someone
Be awaiting us
Be there – to tell
Break your silence

So man's blinded immunity
Be of no more one's security
And with vows
Of "never again"

Be for mankind
To be remembered
If once one forgets
Lives to regret
The now and forever loss

Truth To Live On

You might be gone
but not forgotten
your truth will live on
 to be told to learn to know
of the German Nazi's reign
and their evil laws ordained,
inflicting suffering, agony, and pain
by a country who had gone mad
and condemned every Jew to death.

Truth to live on
no length of time
will wipe out your crimes
we will always remember
and remember one must
so the mirror of truth
be man's just incentive
to a moral life to pursue
and good will triumph over evil.

Remember Me

A lesser pain
Is truth be told
So justice can prevail
No fancy painting
Framed in a lie
But words of truth
As we lived it, felt it
And saw it
Truth must not
Rest on silence
Or it will defeat its purpose
For the betterment of men
Remember me

We carry a graveyard
In our hearts
A load full of broken stones
Engraved with names
All Jewish names
Their last dying words
Are left for us to remember
Don't forget
Remember me

Tell it, tell it
To my mother, father
Sister, brother, husband
Our loved ones
Someone, someone
Must be left for you to tell
Dead and silenced
Don't keep your silence
Remember me

Tell it to your children
And to your children's children
Tell it to the world
What happened to me
To you, to all of us
So that our heavy stones
Be lifted with holiness
By all mankind
Forever to be remembered
Remember me

CPSIA information can be obtained at www.ICGtesting.com
Printed in the USA
BVOW08s2338280616

453799BV00001B/13/P